In *Outside Words*, D outside themselves to the words and power of their Creator to learn better ways of communicating. The practical, applicable, biblically based principles presented demonstrate how harnessing the power of the tongue creates more meaningful and fulfilling relationships.

Laura R. Wright, Ed.D., Psychologist,
The Center for Children and Families

Debbie Rarick has written a fine book which provides help for navigating the waters of difficult relationships. As followers of Jesus, many of us have experienced difficult relationships in which we simply did not know what to do. Far too often, these relationships are simply ignored or discarded and left to die. To the contrary, *Outside Words* gives the reader practical tools for pursuing reconciliation and healing in these relationships."

Jim Martin, Harding School of Theology, Memphis

Dr. Debbie, understands the power of the words we use towards others, and especially toward ourselves. I'm excited about her book, *Outside Words*! As someone who struggled their whole life, having been born sensitive and verbally abused by family and peers, I know very well the power of words! Like many, I starve for affirmation.

Words have power, as her book shares. They have power to hurt and maim us, limiting how we define or identify our self, and to diminish our scope of life. Words also have the power to lift someone, raising their belief in themselves, and inspire hope for a lifetime. If we are going to be successful, our identity and the words we use towards that identity will be based in Christ alone.

McKrae Game, President,
Hope for Wholeness, author of *The Transparent Life*

If our world is anything, it is a world of relational communication! The problem, however, is much of our communication is not as healthy as it needs to be. Dr. Rarick identifies some unhealthy patterns and then launches into a wonderful discussion that can transform all your communication into times of building up, benefiting and blessing. *Outside Words* is certain to strengthen your connections with others!

Dr. Danny Reeves, Senior Pastor,
First Baptist Church, Corsicana, TX

Words, like bricks, can be thrown around as weapons, or wisely put together to build homes and communities. Words are building blocks we need to re-learn how to use. We live in an age of verbal wreckage. Language is used to advertise, demonize, and manipulate. It's no wonder that we no longer know how to communicate with one another.

Dr. Rarick brings a unique perspective to the conversation about conversation. The insight and knowledge she shares in *Outside Words* gives her readers confidence to use their words to bless, to create community, and to have a greater positive impact on the lives of others through everyday conversations.

In an age of superficial interactions and shallow connections, we need Dr. Rarick's words to inspire us to engage with those around us in a way that heals and strengthens our relationships.

Dr. Jason Burden, Pastor,
First Baptist Church, Nederland, Texas

It gives me great pleasure to endorse *Outside Words,* by Dr. Debbie Rarick. Words have power. I can still remember words spoken in anger that the devil still tries to use to torment me even though I asked for, and received, forgiveness for them both from God and the person to whom they were directed. Also, I can remember words that I have poured into a hurting person who needed a comforting thought.

Dr. Rarick has given us the tools to enable us to speak to others in ways that will help to build up and benefit people. We will be able to speak blessings and freedom to others and loose the power of the Holy Spirit to work in their minds and bodies.

In James 3: 1-12, Jesus' half-brother talks about the power of the tongue and its power to either tear down or build up. Dr. Rarick offers two strategies, using three steps, to allow us to use our tongues to speak life to others. It is a book that Christians will find very helpful in their daily walk with the Lord.

Robert Lyster, Ph.D., Associate Professor of Communication, Liberty University

I highly recommend *Outside Words* by Dr. Debbie Rarick. She has an insightful way of encouraging, challenging, and building up the reader as she teaches how to effectively communicate with others in ways that will ultimately glorify God! (1 Cor. 10:31)

Debbie's biblical back up and authentic revealing of her personal failures, successes, and continued learning is incredibly enlightening. This will definitely be a helpful tool for all Church & Ministry Leadership and one in which I will use at Pathway of Hope.

Karen Kelly, Sr. Pastor, Pathway of Hope Foursquare Church and Chaplain at Pima County Jail in Tucson, Arizona

In *Outside Words*, Dr. Debbie Rarick eloquently describes a simple truth written on our hearts by our Creator. There is joy, health, and healing to be found by first connecting to Jesus, and then authentically connecting in healthy community with others. So many broken relationships in our day could be mended by being fulfilled in relationship and daily connection to Jesus Christ, rather than operating out of a deficit when relating to others. Instead, we need to see others as fellow image-bearers of God. If you've ever been in a broken relationship, or you help others mend their own, this is a must read!

Elizabeth Svetlik, MA, LPC

OUTSIDE WORDS

Other books by the Author

You See Me Free:

Steps on a
Journey of Faith Through Fear,
Beyond Forgiveness
Into Freedom

OUTSIDE WORDS

SIMPLIFY CONVERSATION, STRENGTHEN CONNECTION, AND SOLIDIFY COMMUNITY

Sarada,
May God continue
to bless you as your
empower Christ-centered
community. Thank you
for many many
conversations with
you over the years.
love, Debbie

DR. DEBBIE RARICK

AUTHOR ACADEMY elite

Printed in the United States of America

Published by Author Academy Elite
P.O. Box 43, Powell, OH 43035

www.AuthorAcademyElite.com

Paperback ISBN-10: 1-943526-75-3
Paperback ISBN-13: 978-1-943526-75-8

Hardcover ISBN-10: 1-943526-79-6
Hardcover ISBN-13: 978-1-943526-79-6

Library of Congress Control Number: 2016913551

The tongue has the power of life and death,
and those who love it will eat its fruit.

—Proverbs 18:21

We are frail.
We are fearfully and wonderfully made.

—Rich Mullins

Life is short.
I want to live it well.

—Switchfoot

CONTENTS

FOREWORD

Words have power to benefit, build-up, and bless or power to tear down. Each word we outwardly express (through signs, symbols, non-verbal communication, or the spoken word) packs untold potential. Truly, we each hold the key for excellent communication.

People want to be authentically connected in healthy community, and it all begins with conversing and taming your tongue. For some, that involves learning to speak less even if it means overcoming the fear of silence. Others will have to learn how to speak and share authentically.

I can relate. For years I struggled finding my own distinct voice and passion. As a young man, I suffered from severe stuttering, depression, and self-injury. But today a transformed man, I invest my time helping others achieve their true potential.

Like the rest of us, Dr. Debbie Rarick resonates with the human ache of simplifying conversation, strengthening connection, and solidifying community. She explains a proven process to better communication with God, yourselves, and others. Debbie shares her own journey of spiritual, personal, and relational struggle into victory through the strategic use of *Outside Words*.

In her doctoral studies, Debbie found evidence of the deep seeded longing people have for better communication. This commitment for clarity has also been highlighted through her deep investment with various ministries including preaching, teaching, recovery, worship leading, as well as life coaching.

With a vulnerable assessment of failures and freedoms in her own relationships, Debbie leads the reader on a journey into their own communication quandaries. She is an honest and honoring hostess that challenges, encourages, and equips you to intentionally incorporate your whole heart.

The steps in this book have been tried, tested, and refined for years within the venues of small groups, leadership teams, and large gatherings.

Prepare to discover the importance of making room for the cognitive and emotional dynamics of others, as well as voicing your own. You will find a safe place to express your own outside words and the fulfillment that can be found through rightly relating to God.

Although simple, these steps require effort and commitment as all goals worth pursuing do.

Debbie serves as a thoughtful guide, an empowering coach, and an experienced communicator. If you take advantage of the questions within each chapter you will gain greater personal clarity. This newfound freedom will equip you for better interpersonal communication and relating with others.

Kary Oberbrunner, author of *Elixir Project*,
Day Job to Dream Job, *The Deeper Path*, and *Your Secret Name*

INTRODUCTION

CLARIFICATION

ACHING FOR MORE

Daily, we exchange information through text, email, messaging, Facebook, Linked In, and countless other electronic media. Let's face it. Unique to those alive in our day, we are highly engaged in the age of technology.

We are more connected than ever, or are we? We have more ways to communicate, but do we have stronger community?

Our availability to others has increased. We are more accessible than we have been in any other era. But, do we have better conversation, connection, and community?

Some of the hyper-available 24/7 technology has actually diminished, and in some ways demolished the authenticity of relating. After all, no one can completely, one hundred percent genuinely be present to others all the time.

Much relating has become less personal and is not able to provide sincere connection. The hunger for true community (promised though virtual relating) has drawn many into social media addictions as individuals search for personal acknowledgement and validation they long for.

Yet, the human soul still aches for genuine conversation that leads to healthy connection and community. Those who seek to use social media to fulfill their heart-felt needs can find themselves frustrated when the promise for community falls short and leaves longings unfulfilled.

When gnawing desires remain, many people re-engage in the cycle and once again simply try harder to be seen, heard, and validated through virtual relating.

Social media overwhelms me. I can get lost in it for hours at a time without ever accomplishing my purpose. I do not use this type of relating often. I am not afraid of electronic media. I am just not into using it as a relationship tool.

I cannot effectively relate to other people electronically while remaining present and authentic. Virtual relating does not work for me. It is not well with my soul. On the other hand, personal relating does work for me. It is well with my soul.

Let's sit down over coffee, tea, a smoothie, or whatever else you prefer, and let's look at and engage with each other. Use your outside words to tell me about you, and give me space to use my outside words so I can fill you in on my life.

It is important to me to be able to share life while actually being together whenever possible. Yet, moving past my preferences, I slowly mature my virtual conversations and connecting in attempts to build authentic online communities of healthy relating.

There is more than just lack of community compounded by the reality of less authentic connection in this age of technology. There also is what I refer to as "virtual *vampiring*"©. Virtual Vampiring occurs when people suck the life out of others through electronic means, such as email, text, blogs, and Facebook. In some ways, this is a micro version of internet trolling.

Sometimes, people put out electronic fangs and strike at one point in time from the safety of their home, office, or other distant location. They vent. They accuse. They threaten. They self-justify. They blame, shame, and play other word games… then they hit "send" and off it goes! Bombs away!

Though it is convenient for them, it can be quite confusing for others.

This behavior may give a temporal false sense of power or self protection to the one who virtually vampires. However, it can be devastating for those who, at a later date and without warning, open their email or text only to receive one sided argument and assault.

Have you had the experience where someone chose to emotionally throw up all over you, yet they refrain from being there in person, or from being present in any way to do the hard work of conversing?

Something that was convenient for one person can be confusing, frustrating, and painful for the other. As a result, potential for conversation, connection and community have been sabotaged.

So, what is the answer to this struggle for better virtual or in person communicating? The solution is as multifaceted as the problem. However, I am convinced that part of the solution is found in the strategies and steps of *Outside Words*.

The process of *Outside Words* can be found throughout the Bible. *Outside Words* simply involves strategically speaking our words out loud in order to rightly relate to God, to ourselves, and to other people. The biblical principles of *Outside Words* will empower you to put an end to blame, shame, and other word games by strategically speaking your words out loud.

Outside Words includes all communication that is outwardly expressed. This includes any form of outward conversing such as voice, gestures, sign language, body language, or the lack there of.

In this book, I unpack two strategies of *Outside Words*, and teach three simple steps how to incorporate this into your daily life. Following the concepts of *Outside Words* will help put an end to and drive a stake through the heart of any temptations you may ever have to virtually vampire others.

The communication strategies of *Outside Words* will benefit genuine personal relating in various ways. They also enhance electronic communication so that virtual conversations, connections, and communities can become more authentic, as well.

This book is designed as a tool for your own journey of incorporating *Outside Words* in everyday settings. Be sure to highlight and make personal notes on the pages of this book. Each chapter includes a "What About You?" coaching section. Be sure to make use of the break in the chapter reading to record personal reflections.

You also can make use of the companion resource, the *Outside Words Journal*, created with your journey in mind. In it, you will find tools and more space to express your own outside words.

In Part One: The Hurt, we will look a little deeper into the struggle to effectively communicate and the resulting lack of connecting and community in our day, as well as the pain and problems it can cause. This will prepare us to delve into solutions for this timely communication quandary.

Some of the book is written in first person singular as I share pain and healing, struggles and successes from my own journey. Other times, I engage you personally as I ask direct questions that only you can answer. Most of this book is written in first person plural as we journey together.

Get ready to travel with me as I utilize my outside words in written form to lead our adventure together through this process. I will interact with you along the way as creatively as I can.

PART ONE
THE HURT

Irritation
Talking on Eggshells

Look into the pain, don't just look past it.
Stare it in the face.

Two Conversations

Within the last year, I had two separate conversations that were similar, and yet vastly different from each other. These conversations were with different individuals, less than a week apart, in separate settings, and involved just myself and the other person.

In each conversation, the similar aspect that linked them, not to each other, but linked them in my mind was blatantly clear. They were each discussions about trouble in the respective relationship.

In one conversation, I was informed, "I feel like I have to walk on egg shells when I am around you, Debbie." The statement did not surprise me because I also was able to honestly express that I, too felt as if I resorted to walking on eggshells when near them.

The exact sentiment was expressed to me in nearly the same vernacular in the other, non-related conversation which took place less than a week later in a different setting with a different person.

Once again, I realized and also related that I, too, felt the same struggle when I was around them.

From two extremely different relational dynamics and conversations, within a week of each other, it was exposed that both parties felt they had to walk on eggshells around the other. Common to each conversation is the fact that all involved profess to be followers of Christ and hold to biblical teachings on community.

This painful and frustrating eye-opening experience evidenced to me how important clear communication is in relationships. The sinking feeling in my gut was the final push for me to be present and face the relational problems. It was also the motivation I needed to sit down and write *Outside Words*.

Information and Understanding

If all I do is communicate facts and/or figures to another person, then in theory, the relationship factor should not matter, just the sharing of information. But, this is not what real relating is about.

We are not computers or robots. We are human beings created in the image of our relational Creator. Even with a simple exchange of information, the connecting and community aspects of conversation are important.

This is true for the most technical communication, such as those in critical public safety situations or in military wartime settings. However, even in such high-intensity settings, there is more at hand than merely transferring information and giving orders to be followed, and the ensuing following of orders.

National servants, as well as authorities in local crisis situations need more than information to function. They also need time to build trust in relationships with those with whom they serve. There needs to be qualities such as respect, loyalty, honor, and common understanding continually extended back and forth in the relationship.

When I was an airman in the United States Air Force, I learned to obey orders without asking questions. This turned out to be one of the best experiences for my faith walk. I will explain this more below.

As an airman, I did not obey because my Training Instructors (TIs) were bigger and louder playground bullies who simply barked out orders and bossed me around. Merely obeying orders was appropriately required of me as this situation began.

I obeyed my military TI's at first just because I was told to do so. But before long, I obeyed because in addition to the information and orders they communicated, they also taught me. I gained understanding as they explained the importance of operating in unity.

In addition to learning what to do, I developed a new way to think. No longer thinking like a teenage civilian, I learned to think militarily. As they continued to teach, I continued to learn to think in new ways.

Our communication was more than just information being exchanged. We were building trust in each other not only for our own good, but also for the greater good of the USAF, as well as for the defense of our country. Common understanding is what enabled us to build this trust.

Common Understanding

In order to build trust in any setting, there needs to be common understanding. Common understanding and the resulting common expectations create potential for people and systems to be understood, trusted, and engaged with. Such connection will happen only when systems are clearly communicated, learned, and committed to by all involved.

The more I believed my TIs, those in authority over me, were committed to the same system in which they trained me, the more I wholeheartedly was ready, willing, and able to follow orders.

It was not required for my TIs to use common courtesy with me because we were training for uncommon situations. However, it was vital that we shared a foundation of common understanding and commitment.

As I learned to trust my military leaders, I increasingly understood more fully how beneficial it was to do so. The ability to follow instructions I learned in the USAF enhanced my relating to God, because I knew it would be beneficial to learn, commit to, and live in the common understanding of God. That is, as God teaches and shapes me to his understanding.

My relationship with God continues to grow. Decades in, I do not merely practice obeying God simply by following orders, though I do still seek to obey God in this manner.

The more I surrender to the will of God, the more God relates to me as a friend who serves him, rather than merely a servant. I am trusted with more information and ensuing understanding. According to Jesus, I not only get to know what to do (servant of God), but I often also get to know why to do it (friend of God).[1]

Ephesians teaches us:

- God has a will.
- God has a purpose for his will.
- God has a plan for his will.
- God has definite reasons *why* he wills what he wills.
- God has definite plans *how* he wants his will to be carried out.
- God is the one who works out everything according to the purpose and plan of his will.[2]

Those who have accepted God's gift of Christ dying on the cross to provide the way for them to reach and be connected to God, and who have called on Jesus to be the one in charge of their lives can find rest in God's will.

The further we read in Ephesians, we gain clearer understanding that God's will is according to his plan, his purposes, and his good pleasure.

Troubled Relationships

It does not matter alone how I relate to most of the people with whom I am in relationship. If I have trouble in one or more relationships, then I have relationship trouble to tend to. Right now, most of my relationships are going well, though not every one of them.

One of the painful and frustrating relationships mentioned above has been an unplanned field test for the strategies and steps of *Outside Words*. In fact, God used the willingness on both parties in this relationship to surrender to the leading of the Holy Spirit in order to guide and guard us.

The process of healthy healing in each of us, as well as between us has been exceptional. Even though we tried to incorporate the help of another person at one time, it was not enough. We needed divine intervention, and thankfully, divine intervention is what we received.

If I did not experience this process myself, I might think it would be too difficult to believe so much transformation could take place inside and between two hurting people. It was only made possible as each of us decided to surrender to God and commit to walking with each other in God's ways.

However, in the other troubled relationship, talking on egg shells continues even as I write this chapter. A major difference is that in this relationship the steps and biblical strategies of *Outside Words* have not been used. This relationship is in a state of disconnect from the body of Christ and is in need of repairs.

I seek and trust God's leading toward healing here even as I celebrate it elsewhere.

Unity, Not Uniformity

In John 17, Jesus prayed for unity in the body of Christ. Jesus prayed his followers would be one. Disconnection in relationships in the body due to breakdown in communication is out of order for God's holy people.

God is greater than human relational difficulties and has much to say on how we are to relate to one another, including how we are to communicate with each other. But we have to join him by putting effort toward this goal.

We must not live in direct opposition to the purpose, plan, and pleasure of God's desire for unique individuals to live in unity.

At this point, there are only two choices in this struggling relationship. First, remain stuck, and by doing so disobey God through being complacent with disunity. Second, get the help we need to have the healthy conversations that will lead to genuine connection and community.

Since this relationship is stuck, it needs other people to come in and help navigate our conversation through the healing process. Fortunately, God has provided the outside words of trusted counsel to assist us. I have hope for healthy healing as our intentional conversations take place.

To work through this troubled relationship is hard and I am tempted to just pitch it and move on. However, it is my responsibility to seek the help of God and others while pursuing unity in this situation.

Coaching Questions: What About You?

Imagine what it felt like to hear during the same week from two different people they felt they had to walk on eggshells around me. Then imagine how much more it hurt to realize I had the same sentiments for each of them. I was sucker-punched with a double whammy, receiving the second punch before I could even catch my breath from the first.

Have you had any relationships in your life where you feel you cannot be yourself with the other person? Take a moment and write about your experience/s.

_____

_____

_____

_____

_____

Do you ever struggle while in conversation, grasping for words to speak to bring healing, rather than division? If so, what do you usually do? Keep quiet? Speak out without first thinking and later regret it? Something else? Describe your experiences.

_____

_____

_____

_____

_____

It seems we all struggle from time to time. If you have not done so yet, please take a break from reading this chapter long enough to reflect on the above coaching questions and write your answers before you continue reading.

Spiritual Leadership

The book of James is clear that those who presume to be teachers will be judged more strictly.[3] This means that in conversations where I am in a teaching or lead role, I carry more responsibility to walk in obedience by rightly relating. Leaders also carry more responsibility to teach and equip others to become leaders who follow God in obedience.

This is especially true in church or ministry. When I lead in any setting, I simply must step out first, carrying more of the responsibility to submit in these relationships.

My role is not to try to get others to fulfill purpose in my life or to get them to serve me; rather it is to see how I can serve them. If I focus on what I can get out of others without caring for or serving them, it objectifies their person and can easily lead to neglect and other abuses.

The role of faith and spirituality in a person's life is supposed to bring answers, strength, and comfort. It is supposed to connect the person to something larger and greater than self. It is a severe perversion, then, when faith, religion, and spirituality are used by one person, to perpetrate abuse on another...there is a disparity of position between the perpetrator and the victim....spiritual abuse occurs when the Bible is used as a bludgeon to force and coerce one person to give up her free will and sense of self in God to the whims, opinions, and personal views of another.[4]

Out of Denial

God used the double whammy to play a key role in my life in several ways. First, it got my attention and I was able to explore the pain in each relationship rather than continue to deny it and run from it. Since this was not how I want to relate to people, I knew I had to look into the hurt and not just keep looking past it.

Second, it was painful to come out of the denial I used to avoid the problems, when I opted to walk on eggshells. In people-pleasing fashion, I dismissed myself, my thoughts, and feelings in order to avoid the drama.

I learned it can be extremely painful to minister with, mentor, train, and lead people that I do not get along with. The hurt from not connecting with those in authority for me is just as distressing and unbearable.

Both my struggles involve a leader and one being led. Because of this, they are each more painful and complicated than disputes in peer relating such as friendships.

The only hope was to call out to the Lord with cries of confession, repentance, and surrender. In addition, I cried out for help, knowing full well I resorted to futile denial when my previous attempts failed. However, since the denial was exposed and repented of, it was time for God's will, purpose, and plan.

Healthy Healing

Ensuing conversations over the next year with the person in the first relationship included authentic and vulnerable confessions, apologies, and forgiveness extended to and received from one another. In addition, there was commitment from each of us to work on our own faults while forgiving the other for theirs.

Both parties were permitted to and willingly engaged in open dialogue as we made room for and created space for use of our own words. I am talking *Outside Words* in the form of blood, sweat, and tears! That is, Jesus' blood, and our sweat and tears!

The responsibility of the struggle was shared rather than being blamed on one or the other. We shared our thoughts and feelings, as well as the spiritual implications of not being healthily connected. We both realized and confessed that until this was rightly resolved, there would be blocks in each of our relationships with Christ.

At least part of my fellowship with Jesus would not be right until I put effort into resolving problems in my relationship with another in the body of Christ. As in all relationships, we cannot do the part of the other person, but we must take care of our responsibility.

Hope for Healing

Ensuing conversations more than a year later with the person in the other troubled relationship has yet to reach such liberation. There are several reasons for this. One reason is lack of authentic communication.

It is impossible to mend broken relationship without two-sided personal engagement. Both sides must have and utilize the space they need to be authentic.

Romans 12:18
If it is possible, as far as it depends on you, live at peace with everyone.

Since we each admitted responsibility in the first relationship, we both decided to press through and make room for each other's emotional, spiritual, and cognitive intellects. We did not want to simply keep peace, we wanted to make peace. We each had suffered in chaotic silence long enough.

We knew that following the Lord's plan and prayer for unity was the only way to solve this problem. Less focused on the past, we began to look to the future with great anticipation. Each wanted to mature and face the issue honestly. Listening to each other's hearts, hurts, and hopes helped us proceed into healthy healing.

Each was committed to walk out this struggle through God's power, and in doing so, we gained greater love and respect for one another. This has benefited not only our relating, but also the entire ministry team. In fact, it has provided incentive and freedom for everyone to practice using biblical steps and strategies of *Outside Words* with others on the team.

Since our relationship was in a team setting, it affected the entire ministry setting. Because of this, it had to be handled well. I knew that many would be affected by the outcome. In addition, I felt the added responsibility of being a leader.

Wanting more than peace, I desired to lead well from the heart of Christ. For me, this was about more than just the relationship at hand. I was learning life lessons I would teach others in the future. God was schooling me in many things.

I learned much from this friend, whom I also was leading.

Worth the Work

The first step of leading in this troubled relationship was the realization that ironically, in order to step out and lead in the healing process, the leadership title had to be dropped.

Just as when relationships are going well, if I was to lead in this situation, I had to serve. This was personal and it was time to drop all titles and labels and get to work.

There was great worth in what we were doing. There is wonder in doing the hard work of connecting in painful relationships.

Simple things like common courtesy, respect, patience, love, compassion, and other Christ-like characteristics were called for. We needed to operate in the fruit of the Spirit[5] every step of the way.

As we each put forth great effort to bring such godly relational qualities into the conversation, we began to experience healthy healing. We became friends, adult siblings in the body of Christ doing the hard work of relationship both in and out of ministry settings. This was accomplished primarily through the mutual use of the biblical principles found in *Outside Words*.

Apologies and compliments were not just given, they were also received. Receiving one another, as well as receiving from one another, is a must for rightly relating. As we each took the risk to appropriately express our hearts to one another, we each learned how we hurt one another. In doing so, we learned how to better relate in the future.

Neither of us tried to control the other person or manipulate the situation. Instead, we each stumbled our way through relying on the mercy and grace of God to guide the healing process. We honestly acknowledged and felt each other's pain, and experienced sorrow for causing hurt.

Mistakes were realized, acknowledged, amended, and forgiven both ways.

We were able to come to the place where we took care of the past, the present, and the future by dealing with amends, forgiveness, and commitment to Christ-like community. Though this was not done perfectly or instantaneously, God covered our shortcomings along the way in glorious ways.

The biblical process of *Outside Words* provided the solution and resolve in this relationship. This same process maintains our healthy relating today. Our communication in person, and electronically has been enhanced tremendously through the strategies and steps defined in this book. Healthy communication is happening and healing has excelled to positively impact the whole team.

In the other relationship where the biblical strategies and steps of *Outside Words* have not yet been utilized, the situation has gotten worse. We have to rely on other people to enter in and make space for open communication.

Thank God for the Body of Christ and the potential to rightly relate in this relationship.

I have hope for the future of this relationship. It is one where we bear with one another's thoughts and feelings, make space for our differing designs (or are we just so similar…?), and learn to benefit, build-up, and bless each other, receiving one another where we are in our faith journeys.

Looking Ahead

In the next chapter, we explore the force of words. As we gain understanding of the power we wield each time we speak, we are more likely to authentically give to and receive from others. Even still, we move ahead with caution so that we do not put our hopes or expectations in another's response.

Each makes their own decisions if, where, and how to openly relate. There is no way to guarantee anyone will enter into honest conversation with us. However, we can be sure that as we become willing to take the risk and step out in biblical communication, we open ourselves up to greater potential to simplify conversation, strengthen connection, and solidify community.

In addition, we have opportunity to learn how to lovingly relate to those who have not yet chosen to risk relating openly.

FORMATION
SPEAKING WITH POWER

Just as God's words shaped creation,
our words shape relation.

Power of Words

Words have power. Whether kept inside or spoken out loud, words are full of power. This is why *Outside Words* matters.

In the beginning of Genesis, when God spoke, things came to be.[6] Speech has creative power.[7] In creation, God, the initial speaker, is the one in control simply because of his nature as God Almighty. God is greater than humans, is the source of all power, and is the one who gave words the power they wield.

When humans talk with one another in healthy conversations, the issue of control will not be present. Healthy relating calls for submission to one another out of reverence for Christ.[8] Regardless of title or position one is responsible to function in, we all biblically are instructed to submit to each other.

> Ephesians 5:21
> *Submit to one another out of reverence for God.*

Lead by Submission

This is especially true and vital for leaders. The higher my functional title may be in a particular setting, the more responsible I am to obey this command to submit to others. Biblical leaders are lead submitters.

However, we do not have to wait for a title to lead other people. We can become "a" leader in every conversation we have whether or not we are "the" leader. In order to become a leader in the conversation we simply lead in submission.

Christ is the greatest leader who ever walked the earth. Jesus, the greatest leader, was also the greatest submitter.[9] Through the humility of Christ and his willingness to submit *to* the will of God, and submit his entire existence *for* the benefit of people, we have the perfect and powerful example of leading by humble submission.

Our selfish goals must turn from ourselves toward those with whom we are relating. We are to serve the other person, not try to control, try to get something out of, or try to get the other person to do something for us.

Even if we need something from the other person, we can still follow Christ's lead and use all that we are for their good.

It is important to notice each of us can be "a" leader in every conversation. Take note that the goal is not to be "the" leader in every conversation, but rather to be "a" leader through service.

This really is possible. Both parties in every conversation can be leaders by intentionally finding out how to serve the other person.

In every interaction, we can be like God the Father, the initial speaker, God Almighty, who spoke and creation took shape. We can be like God the Son, the initial and ultimate submitter. We can be like God, the Holy Spirit, the ultimate nurturer.

Power of Proclamation

As God spoke, power was released through his speaking. Words in themselves have power. It has been said that "Communication is the most important skill in life."[10] According to one pastor, words are the most powerful force on earth.[11]

> Making proclamation is a form of spiritual warfare that is, unfortunately, very little understood in most Christian circles today. Its effect is to release the authority of God's Word into a situation….Whatever the situation may be, there is no more effective way to release the power of God than by making an appropriate proclamation.[12]

Likewise, inappropriate statements are outside of biblical authority and tear down rather than build up. The authority of God's word is lost in vulgar and demeaning conversation. We will discuss this and ways to turn away from such conversation in more detail later.

In the book of Romans, Paul teaches followers of Christ to be transformed by renewing their minds.[13] According to Paul, how do we become transformed? We become transformed by renewing our minds. How do we renew our minds? We renew our minds by thinking different thoughts.

The words we hear from others, as well as the words we speak to ourselves shape our thoughts.

Coaching Questions: What About You?

Take a few moments to let this concept brew inside you. Think back over your conversations from the last few days and evaluate your part in them. Flee all temptation to critique those with whom you were talking. Keep the focus of this exercise on your part in the conversation.

How did you exemplify being "a" leader in the conversation through serving?

How did you fail to exemplify being "a" leader in the conversation through serving?

_____

_____

_____

_____

_____

What has your past experience in being "a" leader been like?

_____

_____

_____

_____

_____

What thoughts and feelings do you experience when you consider being "a" leader through submission to the other party to whom you are communicating?

_____

_____

_____

_____

_____

Please do not rush through this exercise. To explore your own thoughts and feelings calls for bravery and honesty. I trust and pray God will raise these within you as you journal your answers in the space provided, in a notebook, or in the free *Outside Words Journal.*

Speak Healing

In one of my troubled relationships, the steps of *Outside Words* were incorporated and hashed out both ways. As a result, understanding, healing, and growth happened in each of our lives, as well as in our conversation, connection, and community. The restoration power of gracious words was released as uplifting, edifying, and mutually exhorting words were spoken.

This will not happen if one person remains quiet, not giving voice to their words. The power of the unspoken words will not be released. Instead, it will remain inside one person in the conversation. In this, even the withheld power of unspoken words will have a distancing affect on the relationship.

Nor will restoration happen if one does not permit the other to speak openly. Space must be created for both to use their outside words. Each involved must step up and risk giving space to the other, and also risk speaking out into the space they are given.

All individuals involved must step out and risk utilizing every arena of conversation by sharing their thoughts and feelings, while making space for the thoughts and feelings of others.

Choose to Speak Life

We are not able to choose the outcome of using our outside words. Certain uses of outside words have set consequences. We cannot choose to try to control or manipulate people and also choose to experience the consequences of rightly relating.

In the Bible, there are countless relational encounters that exemplify the importance of choosing our words carefully. Joshua chose life when the other spies did not. He chose blessing and courage. Joshua chose to create life and empower the troops when the other spies chose to create fear.[14]

In this narrative, Moses, the leader of God's people, sent twelve spies to investigate and bring back a report on the land of which they needed to take possession. God already gave the land to them. All twelve returned with the same report. With their outside words, they all assured that the land flowed with milk and honey.

The spies even brought back giant fruit to prove the goodness of the land. All twelve used both literal words reinforced by the display of giant fruit to communicate their message describing what the land entailed.

Things began to change as the unified report from the twelve spies turned into a disagreement about how to interpret the findings. Joshua and Caleb stood expressing opposition to the fear driven and fear producing advice of the other ten spies.

By this time outside words of the other ten spies terrified the people. Together, the people used their collective outside words to raise their voices and weep out loud that night.[15] It was a hard setting and must have been incredibly difficult for Joshua and Caleb to continue to use outside words in direct opposition to the outside words and intentions of the other ten spies.

Watch Your Mouth

In another biblical narrative, we find the story of Isaac with his sons Jacob and Esau. Here, among other things, there were unwisely spoken outside words. We pick up the story as older brother Esau came in and sold his birthright to younger brother Jacob for a bowl of stew,[16] a bowl of porridge, a sandwich, a combo meal.

Esau used his outside words and actually said his birthright was worth nothing to him because he was about to die. "Look, I am about to die," Esau said. "What good is the birthright to me?"[17]

Did you hear that? He actually spoke and used his outside words to say that he was going to die just after he stated he was famished.

Picture it. Esau, the hunter (who hunts for food), was so famished when he came in from the open country that he said he was going to die if he did not eat immediately. I have only been hunting once or twice in my life. However, it seems to me that perhaps Esau used his outside words to speak irrationally.

It would not surprise me if he were tired, frustrated, discouraged, or maybe even embarrassed. I imagine that it was not very often that his expeditions in the country showed little to no food. Esau, the hunter, could not even feed himself with the little (if any) game he caught. Surely, this was an exceptionally low yielding hunting trip for big brother, Esau.

Esau used his outside words to speak irrationally, and thereby empowered irrationality.

Maybe more words were spoken then actually recorded, but maybe not. We do not know. But what we do know is that the power released from the outside words of Esau gave rise to false reasoning and hopelessness. This negative power helped shape the circumstances.

How different the situation could have been had Esau taken time to speak more appropriately.

"I am starving! I cannot believe that I was out there so long without catching enough game to even sustain me. I feel like a failure! I feel vulnerable because I need to ask for help from my little tent-dwelling brother![18] I hate to ask for help. It makes me feel so needy. I better get over my pride if I am going to ask for food."

Assimilation of thoughts and feelings happen as we express them through outward communication (outside words) including writing and talking. Maybe if Esau would have said similar words out loud, assimilation would have happened.

Esau's thoughts and feelings would have become somewhat clearer in this process. Perhaps if Esau intentionally used the power of his outside words more effectively, there would have been no need for the foolish barter of the birthright for a bowl of food.

Words of Blessings

Just a few chapters later, Esau lost his blessing to Jacob, as well. Pause a moment and read this story found in Genesis 21:1-27.

In this passage, the plan of Jacob's mother, Rebeccah, was unfolding. Though the mother of both Jacob and Esau, Rebeccah was involved in tricking her husband Isaac to give Esau's blessing to Jacob.

Sure enough, it was not long before Isaac, the blessing giver, was fooled. Due to Isaac's poor eyesight, Jacob's deceptive disguise worked and Isaac used his outside words to speak his blessing over Jacob rather than over Esau, the first born.

When Esau found out that his brother Jacob stole his blessing, Esau asked for a blessing as well.

Isaac told him he could not bless him too, because the words were already spoken.

The blessing was already in the form of outside words. The power they possessed was already released. There would be no taking them back. You see, once our words are spoken, we cannot take back their power.

Likewise, we cannot go back and say the words we should have said, but never did. As a result, the power of these words remains bottled up inside us. It will not be unleashed until we use our outside words to speak out.

It is imperative to speak up and speak out in appropriate ways for clarity in communication of any sort. No one should be expected to read our minds. I repeat, we cannot go back and unsay what has been said, nor can we go back and say what was unsaid. We have to learn to speak into the moment by intentionally releasing our appropriate outside words.

Outside Words Basics

The basic premise of *Outside Words* is to use more outward communication rather than expect others to read our minds.

Go ahead, invest in the relationship. Serve the other person by extending more outside words to them in the form of appropriate gestures, signs, symbols, and actual spoken words. We need to let our emotional passion join with the cognitive understanding we have gained so we can intentionally speak from the whole of our hearts.

There is always something good to say to and about every person in any situation. There is something good to say, but it may take some effort to realize it and to outwardly express it.

If nothing else, we can choose to speak out blessings rather than curses. In addition, we might have to use a filter in order to refrain from speaking inappropriately. We will discuss this further in the Filtration chapter.

Lost and Found

In the beginning God created. Then, God spoke and creation took shape. Creation was formed because of the outside words of God. One of Creator God's directives, one of his directions to humans, the created, was to care for the earth and have reign and rule over the rest of creation.[19]

Part of what we lost in the fall was the authority and ability to continue to operate in such care and dominion. However, Jesus obtained this back for us. It is part of what Christ accomplished when he died on the cross and rose from the dead.

We can learn to walk out our salvation with regard to such and use our outside words to share this good news with others.[20]

One way that we bear God's image is in how we speak, as well as the power released as we do so. We choose to benefit, build up, and bless others, or we choose to speak curses and tear people down. As we recognize the power of our outside words, we begin to realize our responsibility to choose to release life every time we speak.

Do As I Do

Speaking God's words over myself is a beneficial practice that lifts and enables me with the power of God's truthful love. By hearing God's outside words to me and following God's lead, I can walk securely in him.

The same is true for everyone who does this for themselves. God is not just calling us to him. God is also calling us to become like him. What a strong and beautiful picture of godly leadership.

As we are affirmed by the words of God, we get lifted up and fulfilled. We do not need anyone to be below us in order for us to feel lifted because we are already raised up by God.

Thus, we are able to stand secure in the power of God's outside words over us. This enables us to raise up others. This contrasts any attempts to cut them down or use them to try to build up ourselves.

Whether used to build up or to tear down, outside words pack tremendous power. When used wisely, they can be highly constructive. When used carelessly, outside words steal, kill, and destroy.

Rather than use outside words to make fun of someone or to crush their soul, outside words should be used to build up and encourage.

Hear and Obey

This brings to mind what I experienced in basic training. I remember I just wanted to be told what to do so I could do it. However, that is not what always happened.

It was more important for me as a new recruit to learn the common understanding of the Air Force system so I could properly function at any time in any place. I needed to learn to trust not just my TI's. I also needed to learn to trust the entire Air Force structure.

In the beginning, it was perfectly acceptable to just follow orders of how to stand, where to sleep, when to eat, and so on. However, as the training went on, I was also expected to learn how to think like an airman, not just obey orders.

Most of the time, there was thinking involved in daily activities, not just reacting to a command. I became less and less a mere servant of my TIs. Over time our relationships became more based on like-thinking.

This happened as my thinking was transformed to match theirs. No longer was it about just adhering to a system of expected behaviors.

To some degree, my TI's and I became co-laborers. To be sure, the authority structure remained and I needed to follow orders as directed. However, orders barked out by the TI's and then blindly followed by recruits in my squadron became less and less needed.

This was because of the understanding that came as we recruits learned to think more like airmen. Each day we needed fewer details as we became more acquainted with military mindset.

Words for Ministry

Though serving as family members in the Body of Christ in ministry settings is quite a jump from serving in national armed forces, there are plenty of similarities. For instance, there are times I do not want to have to think, I just want to be told what to do. Usually these are times when I am tired, hopeless, or fearful.

This is common. I have served, as well as served with others who feel the same way from time to time. It is important that we share a common understanding and mindset in our goals and tasks. Because of this, I often force myself to refrain from merely asking or telling co-laborers in ministry what to do.

Sure, at times it would be quicker and easier (at least at first) to do it myself, or to tell someone what to do and they just follow orders. After all, ministry often has pressure of deadlines and other considerations to adhere to. However, though ministry activities need to consider time and cost involved, these are second to the importance of the human factor.

Ministry is performed by people for people, all for God's glory. It is God who works through people to minister to people.

We represent the loving caring God to those we minister to, and we represent this same love and care of God to each person on the team.

God does not relate to us as people who are just to do his bidding and follow his orders. Therefore, we cannot represent him honestly to others by expecting others to just follow the orders we give.

When people tell me to just tell them what to do and they will do it, I challenge them. I assure them that as the need arises, I will step in to the role of boss-leader for the time and task needed.

But for the most part, I will continue to grow in my ability to lead as Jesus did by building people up through things like teaching, training, coaching, empowering, encouraging, and providing opportunity, as well as other forms of shepherding.

Good Shepherd

Jesus, the Good Shepherd was the master shepherd. Shepherding is the key way we are to lead others in ministry. Regardless of what other method we incorporate to lead people in the church, we are always to be shepherding. The care of shepherding people involves more relationship, which takes time, vulnerability, and real communication.

It is possible for me to hide for years in a situation characterized by an order-giver and an order-follower relationship (whether I am the order-giver or the order-follower). This can happen without ever being in genuine relationship, or without ever engaging in authentic conversation with each other.

However, we are to consider ourselves each other's servant, not to consider each other our own servant. People I lead are not my servants, they are my co-workers. If this has a familiar ring to it, it is because it is not original. I learned it from the ultimate Good Shepherd and leader, Jesus Christ.

John 15:15

> *I no longer call you servants, because a servant does not know his master's business. Instead, I have called you friends, for everything that I learned from my Father I have made known to you.*

When God Speaks

Listen to what Jesus spoke. Imagine what Jesus spoke into being as he uttered those words.

- No longer my servant.
- No longer my slave.

We have to co-operate with Christ. Why? Because God said this is how it would be done, which means this is how it will be done. God spoke it and there was divine power to establish released in those words.

If you want to learn to speak masterfully and powerfully, learn what Jesus said and then say the same things. Do you know why Jesus was able to speak so masterfully and so powerfully? It is because Jesus learned what his Father was saying, not just in general, but also in the moment, and then he said the same things.[21] This truth moved me to write a song about it.[22]

God still speaks today and we need to listen for and repeat him. We can hear from God through his words to us in the Bible. In addition, we receive communication from God through his Holy Spirit within us once we come to faith in him.

Speak Powerfully

You and I can say powerful things by repeating what God says about everything, about every situation, about every person. We can join in as created beings, as part of the creation, as those created to bear God's image, we can join in with God as he creates by speaking into being.

We join in God's activity by simply hearing, then repeating what he says. As we repeat the things God has said, we reinforce and resound through the ages and through the universe the very words of God. The words of God and their power will be unleashed again and again as we hear and repeat God.

We learn in Romans that if we call on the name of the Lord, we will be saved.[23] Just prior to this, we read that if we declare with our mouth, "Jesus is Lord.", and believe in our heart that God raised him from the dead, we will be saved.[24]

This passage speaks of two types of relating to Jesus. The first is that of Jesus as Savior. The second is that of Jesus as Lord. One is based on what Jesus does for us (saves us when we believe in him). The other depends on what we do with Jesus (make Jesus our Lord and surrender the control of our lives to him).

God Speaking

God called us to receive the free gift of salvation that he provided through the shedding of his son's blood. He also called us to submit our lives daily to the lordship of Jesus.

If we do not submit to Jesus as Lord by spending time seeking him and finding out what he says, how can we ever submit to him? It is not enough to simply say, "Thank, you, Jesus, I am saved." We must also listen to him.

How will we know when to wait? When to rest? When to move forward? When to study? When to worship? When to pray? How are we going to know how to join what God is doing if we do not listen to his words in scripture and through the Holy Spirit? These will always reinforce each other.

God could say, "Now is the time to worship me. In this situation, your key to the kingdom is worship." If we do not seek for and ask him, "What have you said in your word, Lord? What are you saying right now through the Holy Spirit?", then we will miss out on insight and understanding about God's instructions to us.

To use our outside words (whether spoken or any other form of outside expression of communication) to speak and call on the name of the Lord is powerful. It is more powerful to outwardly call upon the name of the Lord than it is to just believe. Using our outside words to call on the name of the Lord should be a direct result of believing.

Rightly Relating

In Ephesians, we learn ways to rightly relate to one another. We should bless each other, not tear down one another. Our words can bless one person and benefit those around who hear, as well.[25]

Did you catch that? The words we speak to one person have the power to benefit others, or to not benefit others. With each word spoken, we will either build up or tear down those who hear us.

This means that all words I speak every minute of the day either build up or tear down those who hear them, myself included. You see, I also hear the words I speak. We all hear what we say.

Our words have the power to build up or to break down humans who are created in God's image to become lights of the world. What do you think God wants us to do to one another? Build up or tear down?

In John, Jesus prayed that we who believe in him would be unified.[26] Jesus did not pray that we tear down one another, but rather come together in unity. Ephesians contains challenging teaching about God's love and how to relate to God and to others.[27]

Our word formation, our choice of words is important because God designed words to be powerful. We display God to the world as we follow his lead. Just as God's words shaped creation, our words shape relation.

As God's creation, we too speak, shape, and form through our words. We have to choose if we will use our outside words to build up, or if we will use our outside words to tear down. We cannot do both.

In the past, I allowed myself to be silenced through codependent belief, behavior, and lifestyle. However, the Lord is teaching me to use my outside words for his purposes

Today, I speak out more in many area, such as confession, proclamation, and blessing. Though this can be intimidating, it is important that I pursue a lifestyle of utilizing outside words according to God's plan.

Looking Ahead

In Part 2: The Hope, we engage the practices of hearing and being heard. In addition, the concept of the "heart" will be explored as we learn the importance of utilizing the whole of our hearts in communication.

In the next chapter, we will dig a little deeper into authentic conversation. We will look into the importance of getting past anything that binds us and keeps us from using our outside words for the benefit of those around us.

PART TWO
THE HOPE

COMMUNICATION
HEARING AND BEING HEARD

To understand one another,
there needs to be a common system of communication.

Clarity for Understanding

Steven R. Covey said it well, "Seek first to understand, then to be understood."[28] This is his fifth habit of highly effective people. According to Covey, this is an absolute must for interpersonal conversation.

By genuinely seeking first to understand another person before we try to get our own need met, we establish and build trust within the relationship.

When we seek to meet our own needs above the needs of others, we should not be surprised when people do not find us trustworthy. Consider the following insight from Covey.

If I sense you're using some technique, I sense duplicity, manipulation. I wonder why you're doing it, what your motives are. And I don't feel safe enough to open myself up to you. The real key to your influence with me is your example, your actual conduct...your example flows naturally out of your character, or the kind of person you truly are...Your character is constantly radiating, communicating. From it, in

37

the long run, I come to instinctively trust or distrust you and your efforts with me.[29]

Without a doubt, trust in relationships is a key factor in effectively hearing, understanding, and responding to one another. However, even when trust is established in a relationship, it is possible for the communication, as well as the motives to be misunderstood.

Lack of clarity creates breakdown in communication, even in conversations with relational trust. One does not have to live long to realize the problems misunderstandings can cause between cultures, and even among generations within the same culture.

Each new medium of communication brings new words and often new symbols to learn. There is this subculture and that subculture, this genre and that genre. Multiply this times all the different languages and we have an even greater picture of the need to pursue clarity.

Communication

According to my dictionary phone app[30], "communication" means to express or exchange words, sounds, behaviors, signs, and/or symbols in order to express or exchange information, ideas, thoughts, and/or feelings.

This definition is fitting for *Outside Words* because it is not limited to the spoken voice. It includes all types of outward expression of communicating.

Having several definitions, "communication" can also refer to the actual message, that is, the precise information transmitted. Communication can further refer to the means or the medium of sending the message.

Some such means include: a phone call, a text message, an email, snail mail, smoke signal, and rolled eyes. Perhaps you have used some of these or experienced them used by others to communicate with you.

To understand one another, there needs to be a common system of communication. This familiarity will help provide clarity, which is important for exchanging messages. It will also better our communication skills.

As we look further into talking in order to connect with others and experience better community, we will understand with more clarity the role that *Outside Words* can play in this process.

Signs, Words and Symbols

Outside Words incorporates using signs, words, and symbols for expressing one's thoughts and feelings.

When we use technology to express our outside words, we need to proceed with even more caution and effort. Because of its form, this type of communicating will call for more typed words. It requires that extra words be pressed into a keyboard in order to communicate more fully.

The additional attention to typed details can provide the other person with information not available on much of our technology without the extra words. The less outward expression involved in communicating (for example, only typed words), the more communication is necessary (more actual words typed).

This will fill in the blanks, and give broader understanding to what is usually transmitted with vocal inflections and non-verbal communication in face-to-face conversations.

For instance, think about communicating through text. Have you ever been involved in a text conversation that was disastrous or at least caused some confusion due to lack of clarity? I have. Even email can be just as confusing due to the glaring lack of personal relating face to face.

Perhaps you have experienced a thread similar to the following.

Person One: "Will you pick up some milk while you are at the store?"
Person Two: "y" (meaning yes)

Person One:	"Because we are out of milk and need some."
	(Person One thought "y" meant "why?")
Person Two:	"Ok. I already said I would."
Person One:	"what?"
Person Two:	"huh?"...

Since only a couple of kinds of outside words are used in these mediums of communication (typed letters, ALL CAPS, and/or emoticons), more outside words (in the form of letters) are needed to fill in the blanks created.

Coaching Questions: What About You?

It is not unusual for misunderstandings to occur even in our day to day lives in this age of technology. Think back to a time when you experienced lack of clarity in one of your conversations that took place by electronic means.

How did you feel about the misunderstanding and the problems it caused? Be sure to add any lessons you learned from the experience.

_____

_____

_____

_____

_____

Have you ever experienced a time that you were neither heard nor understood by someone who was convinced that they did hear and understand you? If so, explain how it felt to be misunderstood.

_____

_____

_____

_____

_____

Was there ever a time in your life that you were sure you understood someone else only to find out, you did not understand them? Write about your experience with this.

_____

_____

_____

_____

_____

Communication is extremely important and is so much more than just exchanging information. There is a highly relational aspect to it. You are important. The people in your life are important, as well.

Everyone is valuable enough to invest in learning how to hear and understand one another. The steps and strategies of *Outside Words* will empower you to hear and process what each other is communicating, and to then respond with even more clarity.

Foreign Fields

Something interesting takes place in churches when they venture into foreign fields to do mission work. The same thing often happens in other organizations that go into the foreign market place to do business.

It is important for them to learn the foreign culture, including the language, so they can be able to better communicate with those they are serving though missions or business partnerships.

Barriers in language and culture can lead to limitations in conversation, connection, and community.

Learning the other's language and culture enables connecting to begin to happen as people from each culture recognize, honor, and join into the lives of the others. Learning the language empowers the use of a common communication system. Trust is built.

I enjoy traveling to foreign lands. I lived in Spain for more than three years while growing up. As an adult, I have been blessed to serve on several mission teams to foreign lands.

I rode in tiny motor boats to small floating villages off of the tributaries of the Amazon River in Brazil; I met, served, and cared for children in orphanages in Haiti; and I served in various ways in Mexico and Israel, as well.

One of the many blessings in my life has been to travel to express the message and love of God through my outside words interpreted into Portuguese, Creole, Spanish, and Hebrew. In addition, my unspoken outside words have communicated through serving, giving, and otherwise practically helping amazing people in foreign lands.

In each of these places, I had to learn different cultures.

Foreign Familiars

I also lived at various military installations while growing up. Each base provided a somewhat different culture to learn because the commanders at the various locations set the tone.

Most of the Air Force culture was the same from base to base. However, there were some particulars that changed from situation to situation. The new culture needed to be learned, understood, and adhered to.

As I moved from base to base, I attended three different elementary schools. In each of these, many things were the same, however, there were also new cultures to learn and adapt to. The same was true when I moved from the final elementary school to middle school, and then from there on to high school.

In sixth grade, I was one of the oldest kids in school. Then I moved to middle school where I was one of the youngest kids. I had to learn a new culture. I needed to relate to kids older than me. It would not work for me to talk with older kids the same way I talked with the younger kids.

When I went to Haiti, I learned to relate the way Haitians relate. When I went to Brazil, I learned how to relate like Brazilians relate. It would not work to talk with Brazilians the same way I talked to Haitians. In each transition, there was a new culture to learn, in spite of so much being the same from place to place.

Learning Far Cultures

I propose this is true not just for foreign mission trips and for foreign business ventures. Learning new cultures can be so broad, and yet so much more up close and personal than at first we might imagine.

I believe it would benefit us if we exercised the strategies and steps of *Outside Words* in every conversation, every day, all day long. Let me use more typed outside words of my own to try to further explain.

Think about it. Without even realizing it, when we communicate we have some similar, yet somewhat opposing expectations.

I want you to speak my language, and you want me to speak your language. In other words, I expect you to understand and enter into my culture, my grid of the world, and you expect the same from me.

However, when I go into the mission field, at least to some small degree, I have learned the culture and can adapt in the way I dress and behave.

With great effort, I try to remember to honor the people with whom I am relating, in part by respecting and joining in their culture.

Learning Near Cultures

Yet, I often set aside this practice of learning another's culture when I talk with other people from my homeland and circles of influence.

This may happen even though I know that if I forget or dismiss their personal culture (who they are, where they have been, what they are going through), personal communication will not happen, though information may be exchanged.

Where is the breakdown in cultural relevance?

Why would I want to invest the time, energy, and effort to learn about and honor people of another country, when I often do not think to consider or to invest in or honor people in my own country?

I do not have to leave the United States to find people with different cultural qualities than I am accustomed to. In fact, I do not even have to leave my neighborhood!

- Why not honor those I live near the same way I would honor people on a mission field?
- Why not minister to and minister with people here the same way I would in a foreign land?
- Why not honor those who lead me, as well as those I lead in the same way?
- Why would I not want to study and learn about them and their culture just like I did for the people who live on the deep recesses of the Amazon?
- What would happen if we began to sincerely get to know people in our everyday lives by learning the personal culture of their individual persons?

These are good questions and can be applied to everyone we come in contact with.

Silence Before God

I attended church while visiting friends in Florida. One of the pastoral teaching team preached an Advent sermon on the importance of silence in our lives. Her message was about our need to be still before the Lord.

Basically, this pastor taught us to be still and quiet before the Lord so we could study, learn about, and get to know God then enter into his culture. We are called to do this. God called us to his culture, to his language, and to his chosen identity.

The pastor used Elijah in 1 Kings 19 as her scripture reference. Here we see Elijah the prophet, who was used to experiencing monumental outside words from God in the form of words and actions.

Elijah was used to having conversations with God that were intensely demonstrative of the power of God in various ways. However, in this passage, God slowed down Elijah, and taught the prophet that he, that is, God can speak any way he determines.

The pastor's point was that we should not look for God in a set fashion, or in limited ways. Rather, we need to be silent so we can look for and listen for God. It is invaluable to take the time to seek God and give him the space to speak into the silence in any way he chooses.

When we just look for God to speak in loud and monumental ways like the earthquake, we will miss him when he chooses to speak in any other way. If we look for God to speak in the fire, and he does not choose to speak that way, we will miss what God is saying.

We need to sit quietly before God and enter into his culture so we can listen for and learn his language, however he chooses to speak. Otherwise, we will miss out on his wisdom that we so desperately need to hear.

Silence Before Others

I first learned about practicing silence from listening to a radio interview where Rich Mullins discussed the benefits of it in his life. At the time, I was a young adult in college and very much into sights and sounds. The thought of turning off the radio and television was foreign to me.

Yet, I was intrigued enough to learn about it and eventually entered into and began to practice this amazing new culture and language called silence.

With the simple flip of a switch to the off position, and admittedly without much expectation, I began to intentionally incorporate silence into my life. Wow! What a surprisingly incredible experience it has been!

The relationship in which I practice silence the most often is in my relationship with God.

Obviously, this is because more than in any other relationship, I need to sit with God and just be quiet so I can learn his culture, learn his language, and learn his ways. I need to do this so I can have conversation with, connect with, and be in community with God.

I am desperate to improve my ability to hear, understand, and respond appropriately to God.

In addition, I realized how much better I need to learn and engage with other people. Since then, I purpose to invest the time I need to in order to get to know people and their interests, concerns, and dreams.

If I understand you and you understand me, then conversations will happen that can lead to connecting and community.

Why? Because when we understand each other, connection happens. True authentic connected community will be the result of genuine conversation. Otherwise, it is just the basic sharing of information such as facts or figures.

James 1:19-20
"My dear brothers and sisters, take note of this: Everyone should be quick to listen, slow to speak and slow to become angry, for man's anger does not bring about the kind of righteous life that God desires."

One of the ways we can better understand people is through silence, the practice of being quick to listen and slow to speak.

It is so important to take the time to learn and understand each other. Another way to do this is though the intentional and strategic use of appropriate outside words as discussed in Part Three: The Hope.

Looking Ahead

So far, we talked about the formation of words and their power as used by the Creator and by those created. In addition, we discussed the importance of communication itself, including the use of our outside words.

Now we move on to discuss the implementation of the strategies and steps of *Outside Words*

IMPLEMENTATION
THINKING AND FEELING

God's higher thoughts
are expressed in his higher words
and evidenced in his higher ways.

Love with Your Whole Heart

In this chapter, we will briefly discuss both our cognitive and the emotional intellects[31] and their ability to enable us to love with our whole heart. This will help explore the importance of thinking and feeling in personhood and interpersonal relating and communicating.

From the Old Testament, we learn in Deuteronomy that we are to love the Lord our God with all our heart, with all our soul, and with all our might.[32]

This command carries over to the New Testament where it is recorded three times that Jesus presented this same teaching.[33] In each of these four passages, the instruction to love the Lord begins with loving the Lord with *all* of our "heart".

The words used for "heart" in the Old Testament and in the New Testament are similar in meaning. Intentionally reinforcing this biblical precept is not coincidence. In fact, it contributes to the validity of the word of God and its cohesiveness throughout.

Both Old and New Testaments complete, reinforce, and fit together with each other. Sometimes they do this by filling in gaps, while other times they do this by reemphasizing the same principle, concept, and/or command.

Thus, this command to love the Lord with all of our heart remains the same throughout the Bible.

The Hebrew Heart

The Old Testament word used for "heart" from Deuteronomy 6:5 is the Hebrew word *lebab*. It is pronounced /la-vav'/. This word refers to the midst of things, the inner man, the mind, will, heart, soul, and understanding.

It does not refer to just one's feelings or emotions, though these are included in the definition understanding of its use. It is important to take a moment to elaborate on what this word additionally means in reference to one's mind.

The use of *lebab* includes a person's knowledge and has to do with their thinking, reflection, memory, inclination, resolution, determination (or will), and conscience. In addition, *lebab* incorporates the idea of a person's moral character, or their seats of appetites, emotions, passions, and courage.[34]

The command to love the Lord with all of one's "heart" is instruction that applies to more than how a person is feeling in general, or feeling in particular. As evidenced above, though we are to love the Lord with our feelings and emotions, we are to love the Lord with the rest of ourselves (including our minds), as well.

The New Testament teaches us the same concept of fully using our entirety to love the Lord.

The Greek Heart

The New Testament word used for "heart" in these passages is the same word. It is the Greek word *kardia*. It is pronounced /kar-de-a/. With the familiar sound of this word, it is no surprise that it can be used to refer to the physical heart, the organ in the center of a body that circulates the blood.

This organ has been regarded as the seat of the physical life. Not surprisingly, *kardia* can refer to the center or most inner part of anything living or inanimate. Less obvious is the use of this word to refer to the center of spiritual life, as well as the vigor and sense of physical life.

Further uses of this New Testament word for "heart" include: one's soul or mind (in essence, the fountain of the seat of thoughts, passions, desires, appetites, affections, purposes, and endeavors). That is, this word encompasses one's understanding, or the faculty and seat of intelligence.

In other words, *kardia* includes one's will, one's character, and one's soul (whether stirred or affected in a bad or good way). It can also refer to a person's seat of the sensibilities, affections, emotions, desires, appetites, or passions.[35]

Thoughts and Feelings

As we can see from this basic study of the word "heart", the concepts of the Old Testament word *labab* and the New Testament word, *kardia* are closely tied.

When the Bible refers to loving the Lord with one's heart, it refers not only to both their feelings and their thoughts. It also references the way thoughts and feelings interrelate and influence each other.

In order to love God with all of our hearts, we must utilize both our cognitive and emotional intellects, while at the same time integrating them together. This includes the consequential impact of our thoughts and feelings on our volition (our will).

In other words, a person's heart is comprised of not only thoughts and feelings, but also how they work together, impact, shape, and enhance one another.

In our day, it is often thought that men are logical and women are emotional. One implication of this is that females are not logical or capable of understanding or operating in logic to the degree that males can.

Another implication of this thought is that males are not emotional or capable of understanding or operating in emotion to the degree that females can. However, neither of these could be further from reality.

Thoughts, (mental understanding, cognitive ability) are often called intellect. Feelings (affections and impressions) are often called emotion. However, the Bible teaches us that both thoughts and feelings must come together in order to collaborate so that one can love the Lord their God with his or her whole heart.

Christian apologist, Ravi Zacharias gives interesting insight on this matter and the importance of the integration of the cognitive and emotional intellects.[36] While answering a question asked by a student at the University of Kentucky concerning whether or not God favors a gender, Zacharias stated that he would not be cavalier in his answer.

> Both are equal cerebrally, but women are more consistent in being willing to let the thought be connected to the emotion. Men like to hide from the emotional ramifications of the thought...both had the same thoughts. One was running from it. The other was trying to find the greatest bridge in life between the head and the heart.[37]

It is clear from the video that Zacharias is using the word "head" to refer to cognitive intellect and using the word "heart" to refer to emotional intellect. Zacharias provides an excellent word picture as he describes building a bridge between the two.

Here he illustrates the biblical concept of using our whole heart. This concept includes the use of our thoughts and feelings, as well as how they relate to and influence each other.

This command from both the Old Testament and the New Testament is directed to both males and females, and as such, both males and females can operate in these intellects. Each must choose to allow their thoughts and feelings to interact and influence one another, thus operating from the biblical human heart.

Your Side of the Street

For nearly two decades, I have experienced the privilege of serving individuals and families working through hurts and addictions in a Christ-centered recovery program.[38] Part of what made the journey such a blessing was an additional privilege; that of serving with incredible lay leaders. This is vitally empowering.

One of the key components of the actual program that produced the greatest benefit to personal recovery in the lives of the individuals participating, was small group guideline one. "Keep your sharing based on your own thoughts and feelings."[39] This is often referred to as cleaning up your side of the street.

Why would sharing from one's own thoughts and feelings bring such benefit? The answer is simple, yet profound. It is important to share about one's own thoughts and feelings because this entails sharing from the whole of their own heart.

You see, one's thoughts and feelings are what he or she has the ability to experience, persuade, correct, and surrender to the Lord. A person cannot change or control someone else's thoughts or feelings. The other person alone is able and responsible to do that.

To receive help one must bring both the intertwining thoughts and feelings that make up his or her heart to the Lord.

By bringing and submitting both one's cognitive intellect and emotional intellect to the Lord for help, one can receive the Lord's wisdom, healing, and recovery in both mind and emotions.

What Are You Thinking? What Are You Feeling?

In order to implement *Outside Words*, we must think and be aware of what we are thinking. But knowing what we think is only the beginning. We must also realize why we think the thoughts we think.

Likewise, we must also feel and be aware of what we are feeling, and learn the root causes of our emotions.

We better relate to God, to ourselves, and to other people as we intentionally integrate our thoughts and feelings. By doing so, we bring our whole hearts forward in order to use them in their entirety while we engage with others.

We are human beings. We do not relate as robots exchanging just cognitive information. Nor do we relate as raw bloody nerves exchanging just emotion such as fear, anger, panic, or elation.

Understanding the entirety of the biblical heart (thoughts and feelings), will cause us to be more likely to consider utilizing our whole heart. We will grow in our ability to feel and think.

We will also learn from our feelings and thoughts, as well as learn how to tame what we feel and what we think. This would benefit everyone.

Coaching Questions: What About You?

Please invest a few minutes and answer the following questions as honestly as you can. Answering these few questions can be very telling.

Have you ever considered the connection between your thoughts and your feelings?

_____

_____

_____

_____

Take a moment and consider this reality. In what ways have you been willing to build a bridge between what you are thinking and the correlating emotions?

_____

_____

_____

_____

_____

Where could you use more practice at connecting the thoughts and feelings of your heart?

_____

_____

_____

_____

_____

How can you practice loving God with your whole heart (with your thoughts and with your emotions)?

_____

_____

_____

_____

_____

Before returning to the rest of the chapter, invest some time in prayer. Ask God for his insight and to reveal himself to you.

God's Words Work

From the Old Testament book of Isaiah we learn that God's ways and God's thoughts are higher than ours.[40]

We can learn great wisdom from the life of Jesus. He made it a common practice to go to God, his Father, to find out what his Father was doing. Jesus did this so that he could do the same thing that God did, and be empowered by God to do so.

Listen to these words Jesus used to answer the Jewish leaders who were trying to kill him because he healed a lame man on the Sabbath.

John 5:19

Jesus gave them this answer: "I tell you the truth, the Son can do nothing by himself; he can only do what he sees his Father doing, because whatever the Father does the Son also does.

Jesus put great effort into positioning himself to be able to hear God's outside words.

Confessing God's Words

If we are going to follow the Lord, we must consider the passage from Isaiah 55:9 and confess the same; that God's thoughts are higher than ours. The plan of God is higher than our best plans. His plot is higher. God's advice, cunning, work, and purpose are higher than ours.

Everything about God's thoughts is higher than my thoughts and higher than your thoughts.

This verse also tells us that God's ways are higher than ours. God's ways are based on his thoughts. God's ways for us to do things (what, why, when, how…) are what they are because of his thoughts.

Until we think the thoughts of God in our own minds, our ways will not be his ways. God speaks clearly about the importance of our thoughts through the prophet, Isaiah.

> Isaiah 55:8
> *"For my thoughts are not your thoughts, neither are your ways, my ways, declares the Lord."*

God also speaks in Romans through the former religiously driven Saul, turned Paul.

> Romans 12:1-2
> *Therefore, I urge you, brother, in view of God's mercy, to offer your bodies as a living sacrifice, holy and pleasing to God- this is your spiritual act of worship. Do not conform any longer to the pattern of this world, but be transformed by the renewing of your mind. Then you will be able to test and approve what God's will is-his good, pleasing and perfect will.*

We know from Romans 12:1-2 we should no longer live according to the ways of the world (which are there because of the thoughts of the world). Rather we are to be renewed in our minds by thinking the things of God. This transforms us from the thoughts and ways of the world toward the thoughts and ways of God.

The author of Romans calls us to do this in order to know what God's will is; his good, pleasing, and perfect will. Our way of life will be transformed as we renew our mind toward the things of God's mind, that is, toward things that are good, pleasing, and perfect.

Seeking God's Heart

Since the mind and feelings are both part of the heart, we must seek out the things of God's heart just like Jesus did. As we renew our hearts (thoughts and emotions) on the things of God's heart (God's thoughts and feelings), our ways of life will change.

- God's ways come from his thoughts, which are higher than our thoughts.
- God's words come from God's thoughts, as well.
- God's words are higher than your words and higher than my words because they come from his thoughts, which are higher than our thoughts.
- God's higher thoughts are expressed in his higher words and they are experienced in his higher ways.

Isaiah 55 continues to record the words of God.

Isaiah 55:10-11
"As the rain and the snow come down from heaven, and do not return to it without watering the earth and making it bud and flourish, so that it yields seed for the sower and bread for the eater, so is my word that goes out from my mouth: It will not return to me empty, but will accomplish what I desire and achieve the purpose for which I sent it."

We discussed in the Formation chapter the power words have as evidenced when God spoke to shape creation. His spoken words carried more than meaning. They also displayed transformative power. Isaiah exemplifies this.

Speaking with Power

In the first chapter of Genesis God spoke the Hebrew word *hayah*, typically translated as "let there be" in English. The definition is to exist, to become, or to come to pass. The word Jehovah (often written "the LORD" as in Genesis 2:4) means the self-Existent or Eternal and is formed from this word.

Here we learn something extremely telling from the first time God spoke in scripture.

> Genesis 1:3
> *And God said, "Let there be light," and there was light.*

Just prior to *hayah* is the word *'amar*, the Hebrew word meaning to say or to speak. God spoke (*'amar, said*) and assured that what he said (in this case, light) would come to be (*hayah, let there be*). What God spoke (light) did come into being.[41]

This, the first time God shaped creation by using his outside words set at least a couple of precedents. First, God would shape the rest of creation with the power of his spoken words.

This is evidenced by the lack of the word for "let there be" in the following Hebrew text after *hayah* is used the first time God spoke. There is no need to repeat the word *hayah* each time because the precedent was established. God would develop creation through the power of his spoken words.

The second precedent is whenever God speaks (not just in the first chapter of Genesis), whatever God speaks would be creatively released through the power of his words.

In essence, every time God speaks, the word *hayah* can be understood to accompany his words. We can be assured that as

God speaks, he creates. God brings into being everything he speaks. God's words are creative and proactive.

Speaking With Purpose

When God speaks, he creates and then he sends his creation out to accomplish his will. The purpose of God's words will happen. God's words are not spoken without cause. They will not be voided out.

The power of God's words is effective for the purposes of God's plans. This power will accomplish, do, make advances, become, bear, bestow, execute, and finish what he spoke and sent the words out to do.

When hanging on the cross, Jesus said, "It is finished." With the power of those words, Jesus finished what he was sent to earth to do.[42] Part of what Jesus sent his word out to do is to prosper, to push forward, to break out, and to do so mightily.

This is just as powerful as when he was resurrected from the grave, retrieved the keys of death and the grave, then and ascended to heaven leading captives in his train.[43]

Like Jesus, we should be engaged in healing and setting captives free with the power released as we speak. We must choose to use our outside words for the purposes of God's Kingdom.

The implementation of *Outside Words* is not license to use the power of our outward communication to harm people. We cannot imitate God if we use our outside words to hurt others. Please do not hear license to be cruel, inconsiderate, or to even be passively or actively aggressive. This is neither permission nor encouragement to be a jerk.

God put his own thoughts and feelings into his outside words and he said they are higher than ours. As we imitate God by implementing our thoughts and our feelings into outside words, we must be submitted to the Lord following the pattern Jesus set before us.

Shhhhh......

We will be amazed at what we can hear when silent. When we are quiet before the Lord, we gain an incredible amount of understanding (even about ourselves). We will not understand God or others unless we first invest time and effort to listen.

So, we must be intentional about this. How do we learn to listen? One of the ways we can learn to listen is to practice silence as discussed earlier.

Likewise, we gain so much more understanding about God through this spiritual discipline of just sitting with him waiting to hear from him. There is much to gain as we listen to what God says and let it sink in to inform and shape the thoughts and feelings of our own hearts.

Though God has taught us to think, feel, and relate for his glory, the enemy of our hearts is determined to cause us to doubt and not believe God. There are reasons why a person's head and /or heart may be hardened.

The devil knows that if we rightly think and feel, then we will be able to rightly decide. God would receive glory from every decision we make.

- Of course our already defeated foe wants our heads hard.
- Of course he wants our hearts hard.

The practice of *Outside Words* causes us to slow down and wait upon the Lord. We actually invest time and effort to seek and then to listen to him. The more we hear God's words, the more we are transformed. Our trust in God grows as we take steps of faith while we walk in the power of his outside words.

Powerful Prayers

We find God is faithful to his words. Each time God proves that he is faithful; our trust in him grows. As a result, we learn to depend on the truth and power of his words even more.

We will never be able to trust what God says long enough to see if it is true until we just slow down a little bit and get into that place of silence as we seek the Lord.

After Elijah became silent before God, the prophet was able to experience God's still small voice. In James, we learn that Elijah was a person, just like us.[44]

This is significant because it shows us this is something we can do. It is not reserved only for the super saints of old. Just like Elijah, we can hear the words of God and experience their power in our lives and prayers today.

Elijah prayed and it did not rain for three-and-a-half years, then Elijah prayed again and it rained.[45] When was the last time the words of your prayers were that powerful? Mine have yet to be that powerful, but, they can be. So can yours.

Think about it, and as you do, begin and continue to allow your feelings and thoughts to mingle and influence each other. Go ahead. Engage your whole heart.

Elijah was human, just like us. How did the words of Elijah's prayers have enough power to make the rain stop for three and a half years, and then cause it to rain again?

Elijah learned the importance of being silent before God, listening for God's voice. The prophet listened for God's outside words. We must do the same.

Repeating God's Words

Once Elijah heard the words of God, he simply repeated them. Jesus did the same thing. Since words pack power and are part of one's work, it is clear that Jesus' words were the words of God. We know, according to Jesus' words, God's work was being carried out. This is what Jesus explained to his disciples.

John 14:10
"Don't you believe that I am in the Father, and that the Father is in me? The words I say to you are not just my own. Rather, it is the Father, living in me, who is doing his work."

In other words, as we learned from Isaiah, God's words have power and do not return void. God works in part through the power released as he speaks words. Jesus invested time sitting before God so that he could hear God's words. As a result of Jesus' practice of listening,

Once God's words were heard, Jesus could repeat them. He could speak them. By repeating God's words, Jesus joined in doing God's work though God's power. Elijah did the same thing. As followers of Christ, we can do so today.

If we quiet ourselves before God and listen to his outside words, then we can glorify God by speaking his very own words. In doing this we actually speak words which are packed with power to accomplish God's good, pleasing, and perfect will.

Jesus humbled himself and postured himself in dependence upon God. Through God's power we can do the same. We must do the same.

Looking Ahead

In Part 3: The Help, we will encounter both the strategies and steps of *Outside Words*. In order to end blame, shame, and other word games in everyday conversations, we must begin by hearing God. We will explore this further in the next chapter, which covers the first strategy, Foundation.

For successful implementation of *Outside Words*, it is important to first posture ourselves in a Christ-like place of humility.[46] James teaches us that when we humble ourselves before the Lord, he will lift us up.[47] The Bible further says that anyone who exalts themselves will be resisted by God.[48] The choice is up to each of us.

PART THREE
THE HELP

FOUNDATION

THE BEGINNING
WITH GOD STRATEGY

I find God more when I am on the beach
because I seek God more when I am on the beach.

Strategization

S trategization is a rare word with a very common concept
having to do with critical effort. That means it is key,
vital, calculated, diplomatic, decisive, deliberate, planned,
tactical, and strategic as it engages in or with something.

Strategy may bring thoughts of fighting, war, broken relationships in your past, or current troubled relationships like my
relationship with trouble that I hope to work through.

Though the above mentioned types of conflict are very different from each other, they have this in common; they all require
more than the implementation of new ideas. That is, they all
need more than just something else to try.

A strategy is needed by which to work out the alternative,
the new ideas of relating. Strategization is called for to overcome
the battle and bring peace to troubled relationships regardless of
level of dysfunction or relational dynamics.

Battle for Unity

In my troubled relationship, though I battle, I do not fight against the other person. It is against the enemy of the human soul that I war. Jesus exposed the enemy as a thief who has come to only steal, kill, and destroy. [49] This is in direct opposition to the abundant life Jesus came to bring.[50]

The devil, the enemy of our souls, does not want us to be united with each other in any way. He works to resist our cooperation in any forward moving strategy. On the other hand, Jesus prayed for our unity,[51] that we would be one. This gives hope to those of us in relational trials.

Just prior to Jesus' death, his concern and prayer for himself was that he would glorify God.[52]

Jesus also used his outside words to voice a prayer for his followers, both present and future. Jesus prayed that we would be protected from the evil one,[53] that God would sanctify us by the truth,[54] and that we would be one just as the Father is in Jesus, and Jesus is in the Father.[55]

This was not the desperate desire of a man facing death. This was the heartfelt prayer of Jesus, who only said what he heard his Father say. To be sure, the outside words of the prayer for unity that Jesus prayed were an echo of the words of God. [56] God wants his followers unified.

One Unified God

Hear the outside words of Jesus as he spoke of himself, as well as the promised Holy Spirit:

John 12:49-50
"For I did not speak of my own accord, but the Father who sent me commanded me what to say and how to say it. I know that his command leads to eternal life. So whatever I say is just what the Father has told me to say."

John 16:13-14

"But when he, the Spirit of truth comes, he will guide you into all the truth. He will not speak on his own; he will speak only what he hears, and he will tell you what is yet to come. He will glorify me by taking what is mine and making it known to you."

We can be sure that whatever the Holy Spirit says, he hears from Jesus; and whatever Jesus says (including what he speaks to the Holy Spirit) he hears from God. The words of Jesus are the very words and work of God, as are the words of the Holy Spirit.

John 14:10

"Don't you believe that I am in the Father, and that the Father is in me? The words I say to you are not just my own. Rather, it is the Father, living in me, who is doing his work."

Remember the power of the spoken word. The enemy tries to keep believers from unity by breaking down conversation, connection, and community on many fronts. He does this because he knows how powerful outside words can be in uniting followers of Christ.

Confusing Communication

Without outward communication, or outside words, there will be no conversation. Without conversation, there will be no connecting. Without connecting, there will be no community. Look at this passage from Genesis eleven regarding what has become known as the Tower of Babel.

Genesis 11:1-9

Now the whole world had one language and a common speech. As people moved eastward, they found a plain in Shinar and settled there.

They said to each other, "Come, let's make bricks and bake them thoroughly." They used brick instead of stone, and tar for mortar. Then they said, "Come, let us build ourselves a city, with a tower that reaches to the heavens, so that we may make a name for ourselves and not be scattered over the face of the whole earth."

But the Lord came down to see the city and the tower the people were building. The Lord said, "If as one people speaking the same language they have begun to do this, then nothing they plan to do will be impossible for them. Come, let us go down and confuse their language so they will not understand each other."

So, the Lord scattered them from there over all the earth, and they stopped building the city. That is why it was called Babel-because there the Lord confused the language of the whole world. From there the Lord scattered them over the face of the earth.

When the people spoke one language, they could communicate, were connected, and lived in community. Unity enabled them to devise and carry out a plan to build a tower with the hope they would reach to the heavens.

They were strong, determined, highly effective, and became self-sufficient. They began to leave God out of the picture and tried to provide for themselves rather than rely on God.

The people said they would bake bricks and build a city with a tower to keep from being scattered all over the earth. They understood their need for connection and community. However, their best understanding of how to maintain their connected community was to self-sustain and disregard God.

Conversation, Connection, Community

When God came down to see the powerful effect of the people's outside words, he acknowledged that unity resulted in the decision to build the tower. God attributed their unity to their use of one language.

In other words, since they spoke the same language they could communicate with and understand each other. The people became connected and they established community with one another.

However, this was not enough for them. They still longed for conversation, connection, and community with God. We all do.

However, this self-sufficient people did not experience God, because they left him out of their self-centered plans. Their power and unity resulted from common use of the same outside words with one another.

It is important to note that neither the unity of the people, their desire to seek God, nor their desire to reach the heavens were wrong. God placed this desire in both parts of the human heart, in the thoughts and feelings of every person.[57]

The problem was they left God out and relied only on themselves. Though they followed a God-given desire for God, their rejection of God led them to rely on their own strength and was not of God.

They were separated from God and yearned to be with him, yet they tried to get to him with their own efforts. What empowered them was unity through speaking one language.

When God decided to break up this God-forsaken attempt to reach the heavens, he did so by confusing their language. That is what Babel means, confusion. Once their language was confused, they were scattered all over the world.

They first scattered, and then they gathered with various other people who could speak and understand the same language they spoke.

So, to recap, the people spoke one language and became unified. They also became self-assured and forsook God. Yet, they still longed for eternity. The drive with which they were created to communicate, be connected to, and have community with God remained. Thus, they tried their best way to fulfill this longing by building a tower that would reach the heavens.

God's Way

The only way humans can reach heaven is through rightly relating to God. Though God's purpose for humanity includes right relationship with God, it will never come about by the words or the work of people. These would never be enough. Rather it is the work of God, and the power released by God's own outside words.

Could it be that God confused the language of the people so their futile attempts would be foiled sooner rather than later? Dashed goals provided the much needed chance to face reality.

They longed for eternity with no hope to reach the heavens on their own. The solution for this lingering human desire could be found, but not through human effort. Satisfaction could only be provided by God through Christ.

In the beginning, God created, then God spoke and creation was transformed. Throughout the Old Testament, God spoke through prophets of the coming Messiah, and it, too, happened in the life, death, burial, and resurrection of Jesus Christ.

Remember, even Jesus spoke only what he heard the Father speak.

Agreeing With God

Today, as we speak in agreement with Jesus, believe in him, and use our outside words to call upon his name, we are saved.[58] We reach the heavens, but we reach them totally dependent upon God. God said to speak, so we speak. He tells us what to say, we say it, and we are saved.

There is power in our words, though not to reach heaven on our own. In other words, it is when we speak one language, the language of God, that our words display his power. This is also how we become more like him and partly how we bear his image on earth.

It is through Christ alone that both communication and rightly relating from person to person can be reestablished. We can learn each other's languages and cultures as previously discussed.

This involves learning each other's language so we can enter into conversation and actually listen to one another. We will talk about this in more detail in the following chapters as we discuss the three steps of *Outside Words*

Strategic Bookends

To incorporate *Outside Words* is to intentionally integrate a simple three step pattern into every conversation. Foundation and Filtration are vital strategies that serve as bookends of sorts to these vital steps. For now, we will explore Foundation, The Beginning with God strategy of *Outside Words*.

The pattern is laid out for us in Deuteronomy. *"Hear, O, Israel, the Lord, your God, is One."*[59] The word "hear" in this passage is a word that means to attentively listen to learn well in order to obey. God calls us to listen to him with the intent to understand him so we can obey him.

It all begins with hearing, though not hearing ourselves nor even hearing other people. Rather, the Foundation for *Outside Words* is built as we practice listening for God and listening to God. For this, we need to practice silence before God in order to be able hear him.

If we do not listen, we will not be able to hear. If we do not hear, how can we know God or know about God?

Both Old and New Testaments bear witness to the importance of hearing the good news of God's provision. Although God has provided a way for us to return to rightly relating with him by calling on the name of the Lord Jesus Christ, we must first learn about this opportunity before we will enter into it.

We learn about entering into relationship with God not by talking, but by listening. When we are first silent, then we have opportunity to listen, to hear the good news of God. It is only after hearing that we can call upon the name of the Lord and be saved, as Romans teaches.[60]

Romans 10:14, 17

How then can they call on the one they have not believed in? And how can they believe in the one of whom they have not heard? And how can they hear without someone preaching to them?...Consequently, faith comes from hearing the message, and the message is heard through the word about Christ.

The importance of words is evidenced throughout scripture.

Ask, Seek, Knock

Romans taught us that if we believe in our hearts (our thoughts and feelings, how the two interact, and influence our decision making) and declare with our mouths (our outside words) that "Jesus is Lord", we will be saved. This is because our belief lies within both parts of our hearts. As we outwardly profess our faith, we are saved.[61]

We simply have to listen to God so that we can learn. The goal of silence is not to hear information. We need more than realization and belief that Jesus is the Savior because God sent him to save us. We must also make Jesus our Lord, the One we live for.

Each of us needs to surrender every part of our life for God's choice in lifestyle in every area.

We do this as we listen to, learn from, and receive from God. The book of Matthew teaches us to ask and receive, seek and find, as well as to knock and have the door open up for us.[62] To ask, seek, and knock are each part of the biblical process and practice of *Outside Words*.

Words may or may not come out of our mouth as we ask. To ask is not merely to want something or to have a desire. Asking incorporates the actual act of asking.

Likewise, the outside words for seek can be in the form of actions that may or may not have actual words accompanying them. For example, as you seek to locate your misplaced car keys, it may be obvious by your outward actions that you are looking for something.

If you were to communicate to others further that it is your car keys you are seeking to find, then others could join in the search. Yet, even without voicing what you are looking for, it would be obvious you were searching for something.

Now consider knocking, which communicates even more outside words in the form of actions. In fact, to knock implies more than just seeking for something accessible. When we knock, we address what has blocked the entrance or passage to a place beyond our current reach. To knock communicates the desire to want to be or to engage with what is on the other side.

Through sounds, symbols, behaviors, and actions we communicate the desires of our hearts. It is vulnerable to ask, seek, and knock because most often these are outward expressions that expose our heart. We cannot guarantee if or how others will respond.

Coaching Questions: What About You?

Take a moment to reflect on your relationship with God. Write about your experience with and relationship with God so far in your life. Has your foundational relationship with God begun? Are you still seeking God? Have you ever sought God?

_____

_____

_____

_____

Do you spend foundational time with God, seeking him each day? Why? or Why not? If not, what is keeping you from beginning to seek God today?

_____

_____

_____

_____

How can you begin to spend time in conversation, connection, and community with God? How can you improve your listening skills as you invest time seeking God each day? List the ways.

1.
_____

_____

_____

2.
_____

_____

_____

3.
_____

_____

_____

Your effort in this section is an investment in yourself. Please do not rush past this section.

Begin With Outside Words

Though outside words do not have to be literal spoken words, to voice our words is an excellent place to start. We speak up to 250 words per minute, while we can process more than 1,200 words in the same amount of time. There are so many words, signs, and symbols we experience inside of us, that need to be let out.

Let me note the obvious. Many words inside do not need to come out in general settings, but in private settings. We can benefit from sharing with trusted people who help us work through life's struggles as they listen to us and lovingly and wisely speak truth to us.

Outside Words is not license to virtually (or actually) vampire anyone with our words or other outward communication.[63] This will be discussed more in the chapter on Filtration, The Ending with God Strategy of *Outside Words*. We must choose words of blessing and not cursing.

In Jeremiah we learn that we will find the Lord when we seek for him with all of our heart.[64] When we engage our minds and our feelings in seeking God, it will be evidenced in our volition; our decisions.

- Ask for God's empowerment, wisdom, ways, purposes, and plans.
- Seek for God, himself.
- Knock for God to open doors so you can be closer to him and more effectively do his will.

Communicate with God. Part of communication has to do with hearing. It is imperative to incorporate silence into time with God in order to hear what he wants to tell us. Again, being silent before God will also help us hear his answers to our questions.

As we hear God, we become familiar with his voice. This helps us better find, hear, and understand God.

We ask, and God gives good and perfect gifts that we must learn to receive. This is also true of what we seek for, as well as what we knock for. Once God gives us something, reveals it to us, or opens it to us, we are better off once we receive it.

Once received, we can continue to ask, seek, and knock.

- What is God thinking?
- What is God feeling?
- What is going on in God's heart?

The need to listen to God's outside words never ends. As we continually seek to find God with our whole heart, we will find him. When we do, we need to listen for and listen to God. We experience God as we hear him. Once we hear God and engage in the listening process, we can respond to him.

Continue the Cycle

How do we respond to God? However God instructs us to. This is another reason why we must continue to seek and listen to God. If he has called us to worship him, then we must respond to his voice with obedience and worship him. If God has called us to praise him, then we must praise him.

Personally, if God has called me to read a certain scripture, then I try to read it and meditate on it. If God calls me to give or to serve, then I know that I must do it in the manner in which he instructed. This will only happen if I have heard God and respond to him as I repeat, agree with, and obey what he says. The same applies to you.

This cycle can begin when I repeat to God things about him he has already revealed to us in the Bible.

I can say, "God, you love me.[65] You are a good shepherd and have called me your own. I get to hear and understand your voice, and know you. You have made me capable of following you as you call me by name.[66] Every good and perfect gift comes from you, God."[67]

Everyone with biblical passages can do this.

Each person can also repeat back to God the things that he revealed to them through the Bible about their own lives, as well as the lives of others.

"I have peace with you, God, and access to your grace through the Lord, Jesus Christ. Because of this I am not put to shame, but rather I can glory even in suffering.[68] Jesus, prayed for unity for those who believe, that we would be one, just as he and the Father are one.[69] We are God's light to this world."[70]

Pay Attention

We must not merely hear God, but also listen to God. We have to pay attention to him and process what he says so we can speak it, write it, or give action to it. This is referred to as assimilation.

Though often used to describe interaction of individuals in group settings, assimilation can also be used to explain what happens within a single person. "Whether you're talking about ideas or nutrients, assimilation describes the act of taking something in and absorbing it fully."[71]

Any form of outside words from God will work to help each of us assimilate and incorporate into our lives what God has communicated. Thoughts and feelings begin to make more sense as God's outside words to us move from the inside to the outside of our beings.

This movement from the inside to the outside of us will happen through our own use of outside words.

It has been said that words begin to make more sense, that is, they become disentangled, and our understanding of them grows when we speak them out loud or write them.[72] Understanding comes as one attentively listens and then either writes, speaks, acts, or draws what was heard.

The Foundation strategy of *Outside Words* is to first spend time with God so we can listen to him. This will happen as we read the Bible, his written record of outside words to us; as we ask, seek, and knock during our time with God; as we wait in silence for God's answer, and as we speak back to God what he told us about himself and humanity.

This will empower us to confidently make God's outside words our own outside words as we agree and repeat them over and over. In this, it will not be our own thoughts and feelings from our hearts that we repeat, but rather thoughts and feelings from God's heart.

God will take the lead in our conversations as we listen for him, listen to him, repeat God's words, and obey him. This empowers us to allow God to take the lead in any conversation we have with anyone else in any place, at any time.

Waiting on God

Sometimes when I seek God and ask him questions, I find he answers me by telling me to continue to seek. God never tells me to stop seeking him. However, God often directs me to wait on him and use the time to seek him more.

The time we spend waiting *on* God can be enhanced by waiting *with* God. We never have to just wait on God. We can always wait with God as we ask, seek and knock further.

He wants me to find him, therefore, he leads me to seek with all of my heart.

Jeremiah 29:13
"You will seek me and find me when you seek me with all your heart."

Many times as I learn to communicate with and relate to God I missed the point when God has told me to seek him more. It seemed as if the answer was merely, "Wait." "Not yet." or "Not now."

The more I seek God, the more I hear and become familiar with his voice. This allows me to learn his point of view and experience the power and wisdom of his words.

Often God tells me to seek him more, meaning to seek him with more of my heart. In these times, God calls me to open up my heart even further and to trust him with more of my life. It is as if God tells me, "Come on, Debbie! You have more thoughts to seek me with. You have more feelings to seek me with."

In other words, with a loving, empowering, and motivating voice God says, "Come on, Debbie! You have more heart than that with which to seek me!"

Sometimes, God definitely tells me to wait. However, in cases like described above, God is not telling me to wait. Rather, God is calling for engagement from me in the moment, but at a deeper level than before.

This applies to all of us. God wants us to seek him with all we have, with all we are, with all we are not, with all our dreams…; with everything that we are aware of that makes up who we are.

Foundation of Seeking God

The Foundation strategy for *Outside Words* begins with seeking, finding, responding to God through obedience, and repeating God's own words back to him. By doing this, we make God's outside words our own outside words.

We listen for him, repeat him, and then we listen further. Communicating is connecting and relating. So, I repeat, we listen to God and then listen to him some more. This is vital because God is the Master Communicator. We can have no better mentor.

God has called us to be in conversation with and to be connected to him. God has also called us to be in community with one another.

We are to relate and communicate in ways that are righteous. Therefore, our first communication, our first experience of outside words must be to hear God's words to us. God's words to us are ultimate and true.

When we each speak his words back to him, and to one another, we speak truth back and forth. From this place of unity, we can speak to God and hear ourselves respond to God. We realize at least part of what is happening to us as we experience God.

I learned that my heart for God begins to grow in this process. It is from this place of intimacy with God that I find my security as a human being. I also find the strategy to move forward in healthy conversation, connection, and community with others, as well as with myself.

Relationship With God

The Foundation strategy of *Outside Words* will lead us to the place in our personal relationships with God where we continue to be filled up with the Spirit of God. We will be completely connected to God to the point where we do not need anyone else's fill.

That is, since God has already filled us to overflow with His own presence, we do not need any other human to satisfy our souls. This remains true even when God convicts and corrects us.

When this Foundation strategy is in place we will be able to enter into conversations with people more freely. We will engage others without feeling like we need them to complete us, thus we will not try to get something from them.

Even though God has given us fulfillment in connection with himself, he has still commanded us to connect with other people. However, this is not so that we would find what we need in them. It is only through rightly relating to God that we can be satisfied.

Not only so, but we will be filled to the point of overflowing with God's love and acceptance in spite of the struggles on our journey. Because of this, we will be able to extend love and acceptance to others we come into contact with rather than to try to get them to fill up neediness in our souls.

We will also resist trying to fill another's neediness with anything we have to offer, because we will be assured that God is the only true source.

Jesus prayed that those who believe in him would be one, just as Jesus was one with his Father. A person cannot make connection happen on his or her own. It is only when at least two come together that connection can happen.

However, we can engage in every conversation with our feelings and thoughts. By opening up our whole heart like this we will be present and available to enter into authentic communication using our outside words.

Openness in interpersonal conversation that begins from this point of confident Foundation in Christ will provide opportunity for authentic and healthy connecting and community.

God to Me to You

The practice of outside words with God prior to conversation with another person impacts communication quality. Utilizing

Outside Words with God (both to hear and speak them back to him) fills us to overflow. This enables us to offer God's outside words to those with whom we communicate.

Even as the conversation takes place, we continue this Foundation strategy through listening to God and then repeating what he says as he directs.

When we engage in outside words with God, we interact with our Creator. Once we do so, when we speak with others, we can overflow from experiencing the presence of their Creator, too.

This Foundation strategy monumentally transformed my approach to relating and communicating when I realize and focus on this.

Think about your life for a moment. God is not just your Creator. God has created each of us. This means that God, the one that you practice first hearing from, is also the one who created the person with whom you are now talking.

As we remain attentive to God during communication with others, we can continue to listen to God for them. In other words, we will be able to ask, seek, and knock to hear any outside words God may share to benefit the other party.

Remember, if we seek first to understand the other person, we must first have our own need to be heard and understood fulfilled. It will only be filled by God. From this point of relating with God, the ultimate Relater, we can then start to have more authentic conversation, connection, and community with other people.

It is imperative that one not implement these three steps without the hope building Foundation strategy discussed in this chapter. The following three steps must be taken only from the Foundation of first experiencing authentic relationship with God to the point that one has been filled to overflow.

I repeat, do not try to implement these three steps without being secure in the sure Foundation of relationship with God through Christ Jesus. God loves you and has your best interest at heart. I urge you to seek him like never before.

If you have yet to seek God, I compel you to seek him for the first time. God loves you and is listening for you to call on the name of Lord Jesus Christ to be saved.

Seeking God to Find God

God will be found if you seek him. God draws you near as you draw near to him.[73] God also corrects, heals, and guides you. God will cause you to be secure in him in a way that you cannot be by any other means. It is only from this place of security that the steps in the next three chapters can be taken.

Think about it this way. We have to take the beach. Through the Foundation strategy of taking the beachfront (experiencing security in God), we are able to move into rightly relating with ourselves and others.

I love to go to the beach. Most any beach will do. However, Cocoa Beach is my favorite. It is a simple section of the Atlantic coastline in central Florida. When I visit friends in the surrounding area, I always make the effort to find my way to this beach to just sit in silence and be with God.

I watch the ocean roll in and rush back out, wave after wave, as I seek for and wait on God. I have received direction, poems, correction, and encouragement from God while seeking him on this beach. I often joke that it is my special portal to hear from God and sometimes secretly wonder if it really is.

One thing is clear. I more intentionally seek God on this (or any beach) than I do in most other physical settings in my life. Therefore, it should be no surprise that I find God more when I am on the beach because I seek God more when I am on the beach.

First and foremost, outside words are necessary in conversation with the ultimate God who makes up the ultimate community: God the Father, Jesus Christ his Son, and the Holy Spirit.

Secondly, this will empower me to move on to various conversations throughout the day from the security of this strategic beachfront that has been captured as I invested time to seek, find, hear, believe, repeat, and obey God.

Get Ready

In preparation for the three steps presented in the next few chapters, look back through the first four chapters and reconsider your own irritation, word formation, communication, and implementation. Also take a few moments to review the process of the hope filled Foundation strategy presented in this chapter.

Allow this hope to encourage you to press through the pain of your own tough relationships and purpose to engage in the hard conversations. You and those you communicate with are worth it.

Today, I experienced the benefit of such a conversation myself. I have already shared about two relationships that were painful due to struggles with communication. In one, both parties incorporated the use of *Outside Words* and the Lord has brought healing and breakthrough beyond my hope.

In the other relationship, we were not able to make this progress on our own, yet I can testify that I was greatly benefited by the assistance of a third party who listened in and then offered advice.

Not only has agreement been made in this relationship to be more intentional about communicating more (use of more outside words) in order to enhance clarity, there has also been some action plans set in place to enter into and engage in future conversations.

Is the pain of this situation zapped away in an instant? Speaking for myself I can assure you that it is not. In fact, daring to enter into and engage in such new vulnerable conversation was actually more painful in the moment than the previous experience of not talking things through.

However, I know that this heightened pain is only acute pain. I need to enter into it in order to press through into the healing of chronic pain from the brokenness of this relationship. Though the pain is not gone in an instant, with God's help, my practice of talking on the eggshells has ended.

This freedom from people pleasing has happened, to a large degree, through the agreement to utilize better communication skills such as the use of more outside words.

As I continue to connect to the Creator, the more authentically I can connect with myself, to this individual, and to others in healthy ways.

The order of the three simple steps of *Outside Words* will help us understand the importance of utilizing our whole selves in our day to day communications.

By utilizing our whole heart first in relationship with the Creator then with the created, we enter into conversation, connection, and community from the security of fulfillment from our relationship with God.

The earlier in the day that we spend time with, converse with, connect to, and be in community with God, the more conversations with others we will enter into from this place of security and overflow.

Looking Ahead

Get ready! Spend some time in the secret place with the Lord. [74][75] Seek him. Listen to him. Believe him. Speak back to God what you hear him say. Obey God. Then repeat this a time or two. After that, come back and we will unpack the three steps of *Outside Words* beginning with the first step, Validation.

VALIDATION
SIMPLIFY CONVERSATION
STEP ONE

Begin to think of every group
and every single person
as a mission field.

Wholesome Helpful Talk

For a few years the concept of *Outside Words* has milled around in my mind. Over time, I have implemented outside words into my lifestyle and into my conversations. Through sharing about this concept I have benefitted from getting a feel for and learned from what other people shared.

Much of this book is from other people's wisdom and insight. I am grateful for many who offered their own outside words and shared personal desires for better communication.

Our ministry leadership team is familiar with the basic concepts of *Outside Words,* which is to simply speak out loud what we want others to know. It is not unusual for one of us to use our own outside words to ask for more outside words from those with whom we are talking.

The practice of *Outside Words* began as we recognized the simple need to use more words and to not expect others to read our minds. We needed to practice making our "inside words" become our "outside words" by speaking aloud our thoughts and feelings.

Together, we learned how important it is to more fully express what we mean. Since then, the concept of *Outside Words* has grown past the basics of simply using more spoken words.

Now, using *Outside Words* incorporates the use of more words to increase clarity, while also using those same words to intentionally bless, build-up, and benefit others. Not only do they bless those we talk to, but they also benefit anyone else who may be close enough to hear.

> Ephesians 4:29
> *Do not let any unwholesome talk come out of your mouths, but only what is helpful for building others up according to their needs, that it may benefit those who listen.*

It is interesting and exciting when people tell me, "Debbie, I need more outside words from you." Typically what they mean is that they just need me to explain what I mean.

Outside Words basics have added much to conversations in our leadership team, as well as in the day to day personal relations in which this concept is practiced.

Regardless how they are used, *Outside Words* will contribute great benefit to communicating and lead to enhanced relating in various settings in our lives. Of course all of this must be grounded on the Foundation strategy of investing personal time with God as explained in the previous chapter.

World's Smallest Neighborhood

This morning, I was sitting with a good friend in a booth at Denny's restaurant. We celebrated her birthday as she enjoyed her free birthday Grand Slam that our local Denny's provided. As we exchanged outside words, she sipped her coffee. I read a fascinating sentence printed on her coffee cup.

"A diner booth is the world's smallest neighborhood."

As I read that, I thought about how much sense it made. Immediately, it was clear that it was a great illustration of *Outside Words*.

Opportunity for relating through conversation is represented in a diner booth, that is, the world's smallest neighborhood.

This word picture includes the actual talking and relating that takes place between those in the booth, in the car driving down the road, working in the office, doing life in the living room, or in any place that connecting happens.

Obviously, Denny's is promoting their restaurant with that quote. However, the location of the conversation really does not matter. Rather, it is the actual communicating and relating that establish the world's smallest neighborhood. Now, let me take this a bit further.

Think about this same talking and relating that takes place in various locations to create the world's smallest neighborhood. This same type of conversation in any location can also comprise the world's smallest mission trip. Let me explain this jump from neighborhood to mission trip.

World's Smallest Mission Trip

When a team goes on a foreign mission trip, or when a business decides to expand to foreign territory, they typically learn about the people, language, and culture of the land to which they are traveling. This usually happens at a macro level.

Outside Words takes this practice of learning people, language, and culture and brings it down to a micro level. It is here in the one-on-one conversation that we make effort to learn about the person with whom we are talking. In this, we learn their culture.

One way to do this is to begin to think of every group and every single person as a mission field.

This can be accomplished by incorporating the Foundation strategy of *Outside Words* in every conversation. In fact, a beneficial way to learn this is by talking to oneself. Try speaking your thoughts to or about yourself out loud so you not only think them, but you also hear them.

Go ahead, do the whole self-conversation out loud. Ask yourself questions and answer them honestly. It may surprise you how much you learn about the mission field of your own soul. I continually learn about the mission field of my soul as I process my own outside words with myself. Ask yourself the following and answer the questions.

- What do I think?
- What do I feel?
- How do my thoughts and feelings relate to each other and impact each other?
- What is my heart telling me?
- What am I going through?
- What are the ins and outs of my day, my week, and my month?

Before we can wisely speak any outside words to ourselves, we must first hear what God says to and about us. Otherwise, we will be tempted to repeat lies and further invalidate ourselves.

Chances are you have heard people speak things to themselves they did not hear from God, such as, "Dummy, me!" or "What an idiot I am!" Maybe you have spoken such outside words over yourself, too. If you are like me, you have spoken words that were not from God over yourself and other people.

These presumptuous outside words are usually in direct opposition to the way God has designed the person we speak over. This happens when the one speaking does not take the time to invest in and build the Foundation strategy to hear and repeat what God says. It is true in my life when I do not make an effort to validate a person.

Step One - Validation

In this chapter we stand secure on the Foundation strategy and unpack the first of the three simple steps of *Outside Words*. Step one is Validation. We simplify conversation as we validate those with whom we speak.

To validate the other person we must recognize their intrinsic and innate worth as a creation of God. They were hand crafted by God to bear his image in this world. They are of immense value. The price of the blood of Jesus, which holds the highest value, is the cost that God placed upon and paid for each of us.

As we take this first step to recognize each person's worth and actually see them, we begin to learn the difference between people and what they have to say. We honor their freedom to talk about their interests. It may be something that we in no way understand, that we totally understand but completely disagree with, or that we do not care about or care to hear.

We can have disagreements about their opinion and not disagree with their person. That is, we can disagree with a person's thoughts, yet not disagree with their existence.

If we recognize a person's worth and extend courtesies and honor only when a person's opinions and desires match and uplift our own, we are really only using the other person to try to validate ourselves.

When we do this, we operate in a mindset similar to that of addiction. As a result, we use others to try to meet our perceived needs the way we think they need to be met.

Instead, we can intentionally take steps away from this tendency toward narcissism. We begin to see people for who they are in God's eyes, rather than for what they can do for us.

This will happen as we first meet with God and hear his truth spoken over us, believe it, and receive it.

Once we have been fulfilled through connection with and acceptance from God, we no longer need another person to validate us. This is not to say that it is not important to extend recognition to one another. Rather, it will no longer be a drive for one person to get their validation from another person.

After we have met with God and received his life, correction, healing, and guidance, we can hear and repeat what he says about us. Then we will also be able to hear and repeat what he says about others. From the place of fulfillment found only in God, one can focus on what God is saying about the person or group with whom they are engaged in conversation.

Author, speaker, and coach, Kary Oberbrunner speaks about "showing up filled up" in his coaching practice. Once one is filled up with God, he or she can show up to any situation or conversation full and overflowing without the need to seek from others. Instead, he or she is able to offer validation and consideration to others.

Worth Validation

We, as people, exist and have value beyond the thoughts and feelings of our hearts. Our worth is based on what God says about us. Validating someone for their personhood must take the place of regarding a person based on their thoughts, feelings, or what they have to say.

To help illustrate further, I will use the language of first person singular, as well as first person plural. These will be used interchangeably in order to go back and forth between sharing personal illustrations while also including you, the reader in this process.

The strategies and steps of *Outside Words* can be used by one or more people in any conversation.

In order to validate someone else, I must realize that, like me, they exist beyond their thoughts and feelings. I am a living being. I have thoughts and feelings that need to be considered. Likewise, others are living beings with thoughts and feelings that need to be considered.

When I slowdown, practice silence, seek God, then believe and repeat what God says, I am able to recognize experience God's image through them simply because they evidence the Creator. This empowers me to still myself for a moment and enjoy God's image in them.

Not everyone in the world gets to experience the particular person with whom I happen to be in conversation, but I do. I have this privilege and it is one most people never will. I get to know that particular person who was hand crafted by God to bear his image in a way no one else can.

This amounts to the image of God in me experiencing the image of God in them. Wow! How powerful to first experience God, then experience God's image through others. I will miss out on this until I follow the Foundation strategy and first seek God.

Coaching Questions: What About You?

Allow yourself to go deep here. Do not rush past or through this section. Take a moment to validate yourself by learning more about you.

Have you ever thought about the miracle that God Almighty created you? Think about your worth for a moment and record your thoughts and feelings here.

_____

_____

_____

_____

_____

It is no less miraculous that God Almighty also created the person or people to whom you communicate. What does this say about the worth of those with whom you talk?

_____

_____

_____

_____

_____

The value God has placed on each of us should get our attention and change the way we think of and relate to ourselves, as well as to others. You are worth engaging in through answering these coaching questions.

Extending Love

Using the concept of marriage in Ephesians to explain the love and care of Christ for the church, the writer explains that no man who loves himself does not care for and feed himself.[76]

This is more than just an example of how Christ loves the church, or how husbands should love their wives. This is also a call to and a description of how we should love one another.

If I love another person, I must care for them. I must feed them or at least offer them something to eat. I do not have to feed their opinion. I should not feed their ego. But I must offer nurture and nourishment for their body and their soul.

It is up to them to receive it or not, but I must offer it regardless of whether it is accepted or rejected. It was God's will to create them and every single one of us. He has a purpose and a plan in creating each of us and it is one in which God takes great pleasure.[77]

No matter a person's thoughts or feelings, or how much they differ or match mine, I can appreciate the person and have pleasure in them. Not a fake denial kind of enjoyment. I can have real authentic delight as I experience them, a unique creation of God who bears his image by their very existence.

Validation, begins even before I listen to the person. It happens as I seek the Lord about them. Having already connected with God, I am primed to listen to God on behalf of the other party because I am already in tune with God.

Going Deeper

Perhaps the conversation will start with surface talk about the weather or giving compliments about their clothes or their hair.

But soon, I can move past these temporal concerns and begin talk about them, the person of who they are.

I can validate them by discussing the important things in their lives. If they have a new job, I can acknowledge things associated with having a new job. Perhaps they are still getting into the swing of things in the new work setting. Maybe they have to grieve the closeness of some of the relationships they lost due to the change of work locations.

Even if I just met someone, or if I am not familiar with what is going on in their lives, I can use minimal outside words initially to ask questions in order to find out what matters to them. This would recognize their worth, and extend validation to what they are going through, not just what they do.

- Are they stressed?
- Are they hurting?
- Are they elated?
- Are they concerned?

Of course, this will vary from person to person. Their uniqueness is not a problem. Rather, it is actually part of the solution. I can intentionally draw out from them their God given originality and appreciate it while validating their personhood.

Look for them. See them. Engage each person about them self. Whether they receive it or not, offer validation to them by speaking outside words to them you hear God telling you to speak. Offer recognition and encouragement to their heart.

Processing Wounds

While working in various ministry settings for more than two decades, I walked with countless people through personal and family crisis. Almost daily, I encounter people seeking hope and healing from non-physical wounds.

93

This is not to say that they are carrying or operating in a spirit of wounding. Rather they are freshly wounded, often with the raw non-physical laceration raw still gaping open and bleeding. We invalidate if we avoid the person or try to dismiss what they are going through.

Instead, refrain from calling everything a person experiences "a spirit". For instance, if a person has experienced an abrasion, it does not mean they have a "spirit of wounding". Likewise, if something horrific has happened and someone experiences anger, it does not mean they have a "spirit of anger".

When trauma happens, people simply need time to process loss and pain they possibly continue to experience. It is unproductive and inconsiderate to deny circumstances and label a person "wounded" or "angry" rather than help bear their burden and help them heal and move forward.

People need basic consideration, care, and healing compassion from the good Shepherd through the heart and hands of believers. For me to diminish what they recently experienced or are currently experiencing would not validate their personhood. However, it would ensure that healing does not happen from God through me in any form.

No one processes, heals from, or overcomes anything that is denied. Listen to the prophet Jeremiah.

> Jeremiah 6:14
> *You can't heal a wound by saying it's not there! Yet the priests and prophets give assurances of peace when all is war.78*

> Jeremiah 6:14
> *They dress the wound of my people as though it were not serious. 'Peace, peace,' they say, when there is no peace.79*

We must learn to recognize what is a fresh wound in people (including ourselves) and what is a lingering wound that shows no sign of healing over time. This is the only way to validate and ensure proper care for healthy healing.

We also must learn to distinguish between wounds and scars. Physical abrasions evidence wounds, while physical scars evidence healing.

The same is true in every other area of life. Abrasions represent wounding and scars represent healing whether they are emotional, mental, spiritual, or relational.

There is a big difference between the experience of *wounding* (temporary) and living an *existence* of woundedness (ongoing).

Processing Anger

Anger is also often over-spiritualized. If I dismiss what happened that led to anger and simply label a person as operating in a "spirit of anger", I will never be able to help them move past the circumstance behind the anger.

Instead, I need to consider the person and what they experienced in order to validate their personhood. Simple attention and acknowledgement can begin to solve much of the problem since it is likely that their anger is over something that has left them feeling invalidated in the first place. This does not have to take long or be drawn out.

From this place of validation, the person can then be led through healthy healing processes such as forgiveness, offering amends, grief, and incorporating appropriate boundaries. To label or dismiss them only causes more damage.

This is another reason the first strategy, Foundation, is vital. When we try to validate another without first hearing from God, we only have our limited human understanding and ability with which to speak.

If we are uncomfortable with another's scars, our own pain may distract us. We may be tempted to see them as wounded even though scars evidence they have been healed. If we lose focus on God due to our own issues, we may not be able to realize or celebrate healing from God they already received.

This is unfortunate because we will miss out on what we can learn from their healing. In addition, we will be blinded to the ways they can extend hope and help to others.

If we label a person who in the moment expresses anger, we will miss out on learning from their compassion, sense of justice, or other virtues involved. In addition, we will not be able to glean what could help us understand and help them process their anger.

However, when we first hear from God, we can acknowledge the person's experience and validate them wherever they are in the process. We will no longer have to try to avoid uncomfortable situations such as being with others while they experience pain or frustration.

There is a big difference between the *experience* of anger (temporary) and living an *existence* of being an angry person (ongoing).

Seek to See What God Sees

We begin to experience God's heart when we see people as God does. We do not have to try to dismiss a person's anger, be afraid of it, or let it control us. Nor do we have to be intimidated by a person's pain, try to fix their wound, or deny it when we practice validating them in spite of it.

Instead, we can care for their person even while they are angry and/or hurting because we know that a point in time experience does not mandate or dictate the characteristics of an existence.

Offer simple phrases to tend to the person rather than try to control them. "I am so sorry you are hurting." "I cannot imagine your anger."

When we engage the person about what they are going through, we validate them. The same occurs as we refrain from putting labels on them and refuse to reinforce labels others dumped on them.

In fact, we actually help remove labels when we no longer repeat what circumstances or others say, or express what our non-edifying knee jerk response may be.

Instead, we speak to them with the words we hear God speaking over them. By doing so, we counter the inappropriate labels that do not come from God. We can learn to adorn others with the dignity in which God adorns them. This is beautiful and powerful.

Even if we begin with comments about their clothes, hair, or other external and temporal things, we can intentionally shift to talk about internal and everlasting things of God. We open the communication pathway as we offer the thoughts and feelings of God toward them.

We no longer assess, criticize, or scrutinize people from only our limited point of view.

Typically, one does not begin the day aware of all the people they will encounter in that one day. Because of this, it is important to continue to seek God throughout the day. This will help us to hear what God has to say to the person or group with whom we currently speak.

Listening Prayer

Jesus taught his disciples to pray always.[80] The most important part of prayer is listening. The most important part of talking in prayer is to repeat what God is says. Thus, it is imperative that we listen for God, and listen to God throughout our day and night.

Even while we are in conversation, inside our heads we can pray.

- God, what are you saying?
- God, what are you feeling?
- God, what do you want me to say?
- Where are their needs?

- What are their concerns?
- Where can I make a deposit into their emotional bank account?"[81]

This can be done instantaneously and it can be done without saying a word. We do not have to break out into a big prayer meeting. We can do it while we appreciate that we get to experience this person, a unique expression of God's image.

We can validate them for who God created them to be, and also by engaging in conversation with them about them. Even if a person has no clue that God created them and has given them worth, we can recognize their value.

This world can be hard and cold. Many people do not receive validation during their daily routines. Our encouraging words may be the only validation a person experiences that day. Whether they receive it in the moment or not, whether they are able to receive it or not, we must still offer to recognize and honor them.

Remember, quite often a person's initial response is not final.

Attitude of Intentional Personal Validation

I once heard a pastor speak about the importance of relating to and disciplining his children on the basis of their attitude rather than their actions. As long as they tried with the right attitude, he was pleased. Of course, this edified his children and gave them courage to continue to try. It validated their person and built their discipline.

In my own journey to incorporate *Outside Words* into my personal communication, I continue to learn how effectively I can show I see a person with a few intentionally well placed edifying outside words.

At the other end of the spectrum, I unfortunately know what it is like to invalidate and hurt the feelings of others. Sometimes, this has happened even as I to validate them. Other times, I did not intentionally invest my outside words in ways that would benefit, build-up, or bless.

The use of *Outside Words* is a discipline that needs to be practiced. Pay attention so you can learn what is perceived as validation and what offends from person to person.

Success is not measured in illusive perfection, but rather in persistence. It is important to have the right attitude; that of wanting to at least try to validate others. This can be tough because we must move past a person's exterior (whether socially acceptable or not) to reach and validate the person.

The author of Matthew teaches us why it is impossible to validate a person by complimenting their clothes. When someone seeks God rather than seeking clothes, the person will find God. It is then that the clothes will be added.[82]

From this we know that a person is not their clothing. Rather, clothing is something that can be added to a person. The same is true for food and provision. These do not make up the person, but rather they can be added to or given to the person.

We cannot truly validate anyone by complementing what they wear, eat, or drink. Validation must be based on the value that God has given them, rather than on anything that God has added to them.

Foundation Review

Let's review Validation based on the Foundation strategy. Seek to hear God and what he says about the other party. Listen for ways to bless them, how to care for them, or how to love and have compassion for them in appropriate ways. Then, with the right attitude and through God's strength, extend the same to them.

At You See Me Free Ministries, our goal is to nurture and to empower individuals in their faith walks. We are modeled after Jesus who provides both nurture (mercy) and empowerment (grace). We also coach churches to do the same for those who struggle with various concerns in their congregations or within their church leadership teams.

In order to do this, we first, develop caring and compassionate relationships with people. Then through nurturing relationship, we empower people to be healed through relationship with God; to pursue reconciliation, rest, and recovery; and to express and extend both the mercy and grace of God to the world.

So many people do not experience the shepherding nurture of God. By taking a minute, five minutes, or even twenty five minutes to care for someone, we bring such great validation to a hurting world one person at a time.

This does not happen if we try to get nurture from them. It occurs only as the nurture God extended to us has already been freely received by us, fills us, and then overflows through us to the other person.

This living water will not overflow from our hearts until it has flowed into our hearts and filled us. It is imperative we spend time in the secret place or quiet time to seek, find, believe, receive, and repeat what we hear from God.

The earlier in the day it happens, the better. This allows more people we talk to throughout the day be directly cared for as God overflows through us. Consider this, it is more beneficial to spend our time with God prior to when we need what we get from God.

If we wait to meet with God until after we talk with other people, we have less to give them from God. We also are more likely to try to get from them the fulfillment and validation we can only receive from God.

In this initial Validation step, we build relationship with others as we appreciate who God made them to be, and we celebrate that God made them to be. We do not just realize and appreciate this inside our thoughts and feelings (inside our hearts). Rather, we use our outside words in ways that lovingly express to them God's heart for them.

A Closer Look

One of the support groups that our ministry serves is in Austin, Texas. One night I attended a fellowship event where the men's and women's groups met together for a night of dinner and community building.

I remember looking at the man with whom I was talking. From where I stood as we spoke, I saw the side of his face. As he continued to talk to the group, the Lord drew my attention to this man's cheek bone right below his glasses.

I can assure you that it is not my usual practice to stare at a certain part of someone's face. However, as I experienced this, I felt God's presence, and became very aware of God's love for this man to a degree that I was not accustomed.

But then, God drew my attention to one particular pore in this man's face. It was not infected or inflamed. This one unremarkable pore was located in a smooth part of his face. I was clueless as to what this meant, so I took this thought captive to God through a simple prayer, "God, what is this about?"

God began to speak to me about this man. It was clear that God was using his own outside words to tell me that he made that one pore in that man's face. God made it intentionally, to fit just exactly where it was. I began to realize that God made that pore with that man in mind.

I had the impression of God saying, "Do you see that one pore? I made that!" "Look at that one particular pore. I did that for him." "Every single cell in his body I created specifically and placed precisely with great purpose. I did it because it matters. It matters because he matters. Just like everyone else matters."

If God was that attentive to him, how am I supposed to act toward this man?

It is necessary for me to pay attention to what God says about others. I must learn to better love others with the love of God. Not how I want to love them, and really, not even how they think they need to be loved. I need to love others with God's love.

Personal Details

Through this, I learned that there are details about people we talk to we can use to bless them as we simply pay attention to and acknowledge them. I gave attention to and gathered this much awareness of and about a person from one pore on their face that I accidentally noticed.

There are no limits to what we can learn through the intentional use of this first step of *Outside Words*.

In other words, we can use simple conversation as we learn and care for people. It is a matter of first giving consideration to the other party we talk with, rather than having a narcissistic approach toward relating. Self must take a step back in order to make room for others.

In Ephesians chapter one, we find a passionate prayer Paul prayed for those in his life who were following the Lord. Paul prayed the eyes of their thoughts, as well as the eyes of their emotions (the eyes of their hearts) would be opened so the people would know three things.

Paul records his continuous prayer, first, that God give the Spirit of revelation so the believers would know God better.[83]

Secondly, Paul prayed they would know the hope to which God has called them, that is, their glorious inheritance. Lastly, Paul prayed they would know God's incomparably great power displayed as God raised Christ from the dead.[84]

Paul knew as the eyes of our hearts are opened and we receive wisdom and revelation of the Spirit, we will know God more. This is the pattern of *Outside Words*. Before we even open our mouths, we must first ask God to open up the eyes of our hearts.

We have to open our thoughts and feelings toward God so we can realize, understand, and receive his. This means we must learn God's thoughts and feelings so we can embrace them and follow with our own.

When we turn toward God through practices such as reading the Bible, praying, worshipping, and surrender, he helps us know him better through the wisdom and revelation of the Holy Spirit.

We also know the things of God better. This includes his thoughts and feelings about others. We learn insight into what they need, how we can bless them, or how we can validate them in the moment.

Ephesians further states that God raised Christ from the dead and seated him in the heavenly realms far above all rule, authority, power, and dominion in any past, present, or future age.[85] Not only is Christ far above all of this and it has all been placed under his feet, but Jesus is the head over all things for his body.

Full Filling

It is Christ that is the source of all things. Christ is the one who is the source of his Body, the Church, and the Church is the fullness of Christ.[86] This means that Christ is the only one who can fill any person I am talking to, whether they have come to faith in him yet, or not.

As a part of the Body of Christ, that is, as part of the Church, I am able to express Christ's fullness to those I communicate with. The more I connect with Christ, the head of the Body of which I am a part, the more I know how to extend his fullness to others.

As the fullness of Christ is extended, the more likely they are to realize he exists, get to know him, believe in him, receive him, and follow him.

Yes! Of course, Christ will empower us to validate others as we seek to share the message of his heart to those with whom we engage.

This is all pretty amazing! But it gets even more incredible the further we read in Ephesians. Chapter two begins with Paul using his outside words to clarify and assure that he does, in fact, know what he is saying, and to whom he is speaking.

Paul is talking to believers in Christ Jesus. Like all people, at one point they were spiritually dead, sinful, and followed the spirit at work in those who are disobedient. Paul does not point fingers without taking any ownership in his own struggles. He includes himself in this description of hopeless people who deserved wrath.[87]

Then Paul quickly explains and lists many blessings of hope we have because of God's love for us. We have this hope for no other reason. It was just because God, who is rich in mercy, loved us and empowered us even though we deserved God's wrath.[88]

God made believers alive in Christ, and God also seated believers with Christ in the heavenly realms so he can show the riches of his grace, expressed through kindness in Christ Jesus to those who believe.[89]

God's compassionate mercy is the means by which he provides his grace, which is the power of his divine influence. If we truly walk in grace, it will be evidenced by the godly transformation in our lives as we live out our faith.

Raised With Christ

Often I meditate on this and try to let it sink in. Take a moment to ponder this. God's incomparably great power was exerted when he raised Christ from the dead and seated him in the heavenly realms. This in itself is amazing and validating, but it is not the end of the scene.

God also raised up those who believe in Christ and seated them in the heavenly realms in Christ Jesus, as well! I do not even pretend to act like I fully understand this. But, I believe it.

Over the years as I have pondered this concept I prayed a prayer like this, "God, if Christ is in the heavenly realms and I, as a believer, am seated with him, then I want to see what he sees." I want to know so much about this and I ask many questions.

- Which direction is Christ looking?
- What has caught his eye?
- Where has Christ focused his attention?

I want to know so I can look at the same thing. At this point in my journey, I do not have a story of literally going to heaven or seeing angels. I ask God on a regular basis to show me what is going on in the heavenly realm, especially since I am seated there with him.

Though I have not experienced seeing into or going into the heavenly realm, I have experienced my faith in it grow and mature. Though I have not seen it through my physical vision, I do have spiritual sight of it through faith.

The Bible teaches me that it was faith that drew me to initially accept Christ to dwell in my heart.[90] And it is faith that draws me to continually draw near to him daily for hope, healing, guidance, and so much more.

So, when I talk with someone, I ask God what he sees, what he has to say. "What are you looking at right now? Out of all eternity, visible realm and invisible realm, what is it that has your attention? What are you, God, drawing me to, telling me to, or teaching me to look at?"

What God looks at, I want to also. I want to see what God sees. I want to place my compassion where God places his. I want to validate others through this process of validating God. Only when I look to God and join him can I be part of the process of his fulfilling others.

Seeing What God Sees

Last month, I was alone in my car waiting at a down town stop light as I was driving to the gym. I took advantage of the moment, turned off the radio, and asked God to show me what he saw, where his heart was in that moment. I wondered and wanted to participate where God's concern was right then.

Immediately, my physical eyes focused on a figure moving in the alley about a block ahead. As I took a second to focus my attention on what God highlighted, I saw a man walking down an alley further down the street. I prayed a simple prayer, "Please bless that man, Lord."

Then I began to feel God's love for this man.

Suddenly, I could see the man stumble and fall! It was not a hard fall, but a tumbling rolling kind of fall. My heart jumped! It mattered to me that this man fell, because it mattered to God that this man fell.

I had to go check on him. I changed lanes, and when the light turned green, I caught up to the man and pulled over to see how he fared from the fall.

As I told him that I saw him fall and I wanted to see if he was okay, his whole countenance changed from one of pain, to one of relief. I am sure his body still hurt, but his feelings and thoughts (his heart) were being attended to through this simple expression of compassionate outside words.

I was floored at how much this obviously meant to him.

I continued to ask God where he was gazing. I had the distinct impression God was looking at this man in a deep and detailed manner. I began to look at this man, too. I began to really see him for the human being he was.

What was his story? Chances are it mattered to few people that he fell today. It only mattered to me because God let me see what he saw in that moment.

This man and I continued to talk for a few minutes. As the conversation progressed, I asked God what outside words he wanted me to say to this man. God pointed out many things to me in that moment, but only one to speak to this man.

I began to sense an even greater overwhelming sense of God's love for him! I tried to tell him how much God loved him. I wanted him to know that he was so powerfully loved.

Eventually, the dear man allowed this weeping woman to pray for him. God also provided the opportunity for me to give him a ride to his GED class, and to give him some coffee (that just happened to be an extra from a breakfast meeting I just left).

I never made it to the workout that day. Instead, God led me in a spiritual exercise to seek, find, and extend God to another.

This is so vastly different from previous years of my life where I hid my heart behind passive aggressive mocking and making fun of people's falls, failures, and frailties.

Hiding Behind My Mouth

In years past, I was too unsure of myself to receive authentic validation from others. I constantly ran down others to try to cover my insecurities. I resorted to cut down fights, and flinging insults and put downs, often in the name of loving and having fun.

Instead of being loving or fun, I simply tried to validate myself by insulting others and making fun of them. It never worked. Though people laughed, no one was validated.

The experience with this man who fell in the alley was refreshingly different from the previous sarcastic pride with which I used to try to cover my lack of confidence. I know as I keep calling on God, he will continue to build my security in him so I can use the outside words and actions of my life to bless rather than to beat down.

As I gave him a ride to his class, the man shared more of his thoughts and feelings with me as he continued to talk about his tumble and share his concern that others might fall, too. It was only because God worked in me that I was able to experience any of this.

The man was blown away that someone saw him fall and cared enough to check on him.

This is a simple example of the first step, Validation. After I asked for it, I simply received from God the direction of his own heart. This enabled me to extend God's heart to this man. By doing so, I experienced someone I may have never met otherwise.

God allowed me to experience his great love for this man. When I told the man about God's love for him, I experienced

God's love for him again as it flowed from God through me to this man.

When we serve as a conduit for God's love, we get to experience it twice – once when he shows it to us, and once when it flows from us to another.

Blessing God

God's love is so powerful and healing it does not matter it was God's love for another person I felt. It only mattered that I felt God's love! I experienced God's love twice. Regardless of who it was for, I experienced it, too! God's love welled up in me, overflowed through me. In doing so, it cared for me, too.

Even after I dropped off this man at his class, I drove away telling God how much he (God) loved this man.

I said with really loud and excited outside words, "God! You love that man so much! You care he fell! God, you care he was not going to make it on time to his class without a ride!" "You love him so much!"

Prior to this, I rarely experienced that much of God's love at one time. I keep learning new insight into the muchness of God's love. This was definitely a lesson for me. Through this experience I learned more about how to extend God's love to another.

I learned how simple it is to validate someone I just met.

God wants us to tell people how much he cares about them, even about that one particular pore on their face, or how much he cares that they fell in the alley. As I ask God what he cares about, I can learn, care about, and validate the people that he highlights to me. This equips me with new ways to honor and bless others, as well.

Validation, the first step, begins even before we try to understand someone. Before we attempt to understand them, we validate them. Recognize them, their worth, and their uniqueness as a creation of God. God loves them, regardless of what they have to say.

This step is first in sequence, primacy, and importance. The Bible tells us to seek first God's kingdom and his righteousness.[91] As we do this we will be validated as we draw from the pool of God's outside words and then be able to extend the same to individuals and groups of all sizes.

Looking Ahead

In the next chapter, we will discuss the second step, Cooperation. It is here we will begin the process of first understanding the other person. Once we have blessed them with recognizing their personal worth, we move on to bless them with attentiveness through interpersonal Cooperation.

COOPERATION
STRENGTHEN CONNECTION
STEP TWO

We can argue with the concept of God,
but we must wrestle with the presence of God.

God of Everyday

The Foundation strategy for *Outside Words* is conversation with, connection to, and community with God. This alone enables us to hear the Lord even as we talk with others.

It is not enough that at some point in our lives we heard about God and merely cognitively began to realize and acknowledge God's existence.

Paul, the author of much of the New Testament, prayed for those who are in God's family, that is, those who believe in Jesus. Paul prayed that the inner being of believers would be strengthened with power through God's Spirit within.[92]

It was Paul's humble, yet powerful request that God do this out of his glorious riches so Christ may dwell in the heart of the believer.[93] Christ does not merely enter the heart of those who believe in him, he actually dwells there. God makes his home in and settles into the human heart through their faith.

When this happens, transformation will follow. No one can encounter God and remain the same.

Experiencing God is not just a one-time event, but something we do every day. We can speak to God today, because he is alive today.

This is why it is important we acknowledge and care for others. We can appreciate that God created them, every pore of them. We can and need to offer validation to the person for their very existence. Not only so, we also can validate how they, merely by existing, bear witness to their Creator's existence.

Each of us bears witness to our Creator even apart from faith in Christ.

God's Image and Instructions

It does not take much to acknowledge that we get to experience this person, this unique creation of God, and witness God through their lives to some degree.

When we hear from God, we are able to appreciate and tend to people based on insight we gain from God about the situations or circumstances at hand. Once we hear information from God, we must then seek his instructions. We need to know what God is saying and why.

God may let us know this person is afraid, and then instruct us to speak courage into them and pray for them.

If the person or group we are talking to is going in the wrong direction, God may inform us and instruct us to silently pray for them.

It may be that God tells us the one we are talking to is on the right track, then instruct us to encourage them.

Whatever God shares with us can be general information or specific details. It can be direct instructions, a simple word, or phrase to say.

We do not control the other person or put thoughts and ideas into their minds. Neither do we try to assert our thoughts and feelings onto others. We must not assume that since we heard from God we have now become their judge.

Rather, we speak to them with the insight, love, and compassion of God. It entails tapping into God's thoughts and Gods feelings (God's heart) about this person, and then sharing with them as God leads us to.

Validation, the first step of *Outside Words*, must always benefit, build-up, or bless the other person. A powerful practice is to call things forward in people through personal encouragement.

We have already received our worth from God in our personal time with him earlier in the day. Therefore, we are free from the need for and free from trying to get validation from others.

This means we do not need applause, to be agreed with, or even for others to listen to our outside words as we offer compliments. Maybe they are not able to receive honor or able to talk about themselves.

Even though we try to hear from God and obey him while we relate to others, it is likely we will be wrong sometimes. Again, this is not about perfection, but rather stepping out and growing in our faith in Christ-like gestures.

Whatever the circumstances, our outside words must be utilized in an attempt to validate the other person, rather than use our outside words or the other person to do the same for us.

Step Two - Cooperation

Once the first step, Validation is in place, it is time to move to the second step, Cooperation. In this step, we continue to put our own agenda on hold and we begin to cooperate with the other person. Cooperation happens as we take time to listen to them and hear what they have to say.

Moving beyond their personhood (the importance of who they are), we direct our attention to information or anything else they want to communicate (what they want to say). As we cooperate with others, we will strengthen connection.

Notice that it is time to *move to* the second step. However, it is vital to realize that it is not time to *move on to* the second step. In other words, Validation of the person continues even as the Cooperation (listening to the person) begins.

It may be helpful to remember the person we just offered validation to (whether they received it or not) is now the same one we will attempt to cooperate with. To do this, we hold our tongue in order to create space for them to speak into while we listen.

Covey taught us to seek first to understand, then to be understood.[94] This happens as we further validate, extend courtesies and sincerely offer to hear them first. We follow up this offer with genuine and patient listening.

God is ever interested in every single little pore in their body and every concern they have in their life. Because of this, we do not stop acknowledging them as a person even as we cooperate with them by first listening to what they have to say.

God always expresses his love to them and wants to do so partially through us. This is important because authentic personal validation will enable deeper interpersonal connection. Whether they realize it or not, they always bear God's image and proof of their Creator's existence.

Jesus Modeled Cooperation

Once we incorporate the Foundation strategy into our day, we have already listened in our relationship with God. We first sought, found, heard, believed, and repeated what God said to us. As we do this, we follow the model Jesus gave us as he too, practiced seeking God's outside words.

Jesus sought, found, heard, believed, and obeyed God. Jesus repeated only what God said. We learn this from the New Testament book of John. To some degree, we practice the same thing as we listen to people.

One big difference is that we do not listen to others so we can say only and exactly what they say. To only speak what another human spoke would not be healthy. However, Jesus only repeated what God Almighty said. In doing so, Jesus modeled intentional listening to and healthy dependency upon God.

Interdependence with other people is healthy. Our effort is twofold. First, through Validation, we simplify our conversation. Second, we strengthen connection through Cooperation as we use our non-verbal outside words (nodding, paying attention, facial expressions, body language) as we listen.

Remember, the goal is for this to happen whether or not we agree with them. Cooperation does not mean that we agree with what they say. Likewise, listening to them does not mean that we support or agree with their comments.

It is not the topic that is validated, rather it is the person. In the same manner, it is not the comment that is being cooperated with, rather it is the individual.

Listening to Hearts with God's Heart

Each person gets to have their own thoughts and feelings. When we tell another person what they think or feel, we disregard them. We dismiss creations of God when we attempt to speak for them, that is, we take away their voice. This is neither cooperative nor a display of compassion.

However, we show we care as we listen, respond, and make comments or ask questions based on what they communicate. We cooperate with them when we ensure what they wanted to say has been heard, and attempts have been made to understand them.

Though we ask God what his heart is for others, we should never think we will ever know God's whole heart for them. We can only say what we believe we hear God saying.

This calls for a humble approach as we offer what we believe we have heard for their consideration. Many times, we do not even need to let them know we have sought God for their behalf. Rather, we hear and humbly speak truth into their lives.

We must make effort to speak in a way that catches their attention and entices them to move toward God rather than away from God. Remember, our words have a positive or negative effect on each person who hears them, drawing them toward or away from God.

It is imperative to let people have space to have their own thoughts and feelings. When we do so, we find they are able to experience God where they are. This happens after we acknowledge their value and worth.

Once a person experiences God wherever they are, they can then grow from there. Instead of expecting them to come up to what we consider our higher level, we need to honor them and authentically meet with them.

Honoring a person's opinion does not mean agreeing with it. We can be agreeable with a person even when we are not in agreement with their opinions. We can recognize the person and honor that they have opinions, too.

This is possible because God assessed them to have ultimate worth, being worthy of the shed blood of Jesus. When we remember God's love for the world, we can validate and cooperate with others as we remain confident in the validation and cooperation we received from God.

Vulnerable Self

If while talking politics, religion, or some other subject we find we disagree with someone's opinion, we have choices in how to respond to and treat the other person.

A temptation may be to revert to self-defense and invalidate others when we become threatened by what someone shares with us. In these times, we may choose to cut them off, rather than listen to them. As we fustily strive to build-up ourselves this way, we evidence our own need to remember and receive God's validation of and cooperation with us.

In addition, rather than cooperate with the person and let them share first, we will begin to try to get them to cooperate with us. We immediately speak out rather than first make space for their thoughts and feelings, from their heart.

Likewise, when someone opens up and shares their heart with us and we disregard them, we crush them instead of recognizing them as a person of value. We do this as we blast out our views on the subject to prove how wrong they are and how right we are. We dishonor their worth as we strive to benefit ourselves.

Maybe we did this because we were threatened by them or their opinion. Perhaps we have no idea why we reacted that way. What we do know is this would not happen if we operated out of our Foundation relationship with God.

Think about it. When we open our hearts to share authentically with others we make ourselves vulnerable to their response to us and our opinions. We should remember that we do not experience any threat (real or perceived) that is bigger than God's protection.

However, when we try to justify our reactions, it evidences our insecurity.

Do we try to validate and cooperate with the other person, or do we try to get validation and cooperation from the other person for ourselves?

If we try to get others to fulfill us, we have stepped away from outside words with God and the fulfillment he brings. However, when we engage God's outside words we do not use settings, conversation topics, people involved, or circumstances to try to prove our worth.

Instead, regardless of what we experience, we will have God's peace.

Peace Past Understanding

The Bible teaches about peace that passes understanding. This is peace that happens even when it does not make sense to have peace.[95] It is beyond our understanding how we can have peace in some circumstances. However, God provides peace in any circumstance when we stay in conversation with and connected to him.

When someone talks in such a way that contradicts godliness while they justify it as being godly, something in me rises up that wants to scream, "No!" Maybe you can relate to this. How dare they use God to justify disobedience or to excuse rebellion, narcissism, or cruelty?

But even when this happens, I can experience God's peace because one person's misuse of God does not have to rob me of my connection to God.

I can say "no" to something that was said, and disagree with it, without saying "no" to an individual's personhood and worth.

Everyone gets to have their own thoughts. Everyone gets to have their own feelings. Everyone gets to have their own opinions.

We cannot dictate to others what is going on inside of them or why. We will appear foolish if we try to.

Part of bearing God's image is following God's lead. Like God, we allow people to be how they are, where they are. This is the only way they will be able to ever move on to become who God created them to be and be how God created them to be.

I need the same thing in my life. We each do. No one can grow, mature, or explore Christian lifestyle if someone is trying to take away their freedom to think, feel, and speak for their self.

When we assess, criticize, and label others, it does not help others know they are loved. Neither does it help them grow in their understanding of the one true God who loves them dearly and is powerfully able to lead them clearly.

As long as we remain in the place of acceptance from our personal fellowship with God, we are able to accept others regardless of what they say or do. But, when we approach someone from a place of need in our lives, then we have stepped away from God as our Foundation.

In this, we have climbed up on the shoulders of another person in order try to get them to fulfill us. We do this by trying to get them to sustain us through agreeing with us, validating us, and serving us. This futile effort is not peaceful.

Stop Cooperating With the Lies

If we do this, we have turned away from the Lord and stopped believing he is enough for us. Somehow the lie that God is insufficient has slipped in and tricked us out of assurance in God's peace.

We know that we are not the source of peace, so we are left with trying to get peace from another person.

Let's look a little closer at the futility of this mode of self-operation rather than co-operation.

When we turn from God's peace and fulfillment, we try to get validation and cooperation from other humans. To make matters worse, we try to get this from people with whom we do not even agree.

It is outlandish the things that we will try to use to fulfill us when we step away from the underlying Foundation we receive from our personal time with God. We must constantly put effort to seek and find God, and totally rely on him.

The first step of Twelve Step Programs affirms the need to admit that on our own, we are powerless. Only when we come to the end of our own effort and still not have the desired victory in our lives do we admit that we are powerless. Remaining mindful of our inability without God's power helps us be more likely to stay connected to and receive power from Christ Jesus.

Coaching Questions: What About You?

Do not rush through or skip this response section. Please invest the time needed to really listen to your whole heart (both your thoughts and feelings) as you reflect on these questions.

Have you come to the place in your life where you realize your need for God?

_____

_____

_____

_____

_____

If you have, have you called out to God in prayer seeking his help? If you have, please write your thoughts and feelings about it.

_____

_____

_____

_____

_____

If not, please consider what may be hindering you in this process and journal your findings here.

_____

_____

_____

_____

_____

God wants to come into your life and help you experience his love and leading for the rest of your life. Ask God to show you what you believe and how to cooperate with him and move on from there to personal relationship with him. If you already experience personal relationship with God, ask him to draw you into deeper cooperation and connection with him.

Validation and Cooperation

To recap, we acknowledge the person, love them, and let them know this is a safe place to be authentic and to share honestly. It is also a safe place for us to be at peace even when we do not agree with them. We extend love and leave it to them whether they receive it or not. We just let the Lord flow through us.

Maybe there is an obvious difference of opinions and the other person is having a hard time about the disagreement. This is an excellent opportunity to rely on God to help us be selfless and express God's life and love in that setting.

Not everyone knows about the presence of the Lord, but they will be able to experience the peace that comes through the Foundation strategy in our lives, as well as the Validation and Cooperation steps of *Outside Words*.

Even if they walk away angry, shaming, and finger-pointing, they will not be able to explain away the love of God they experienced flow through us as we overflowed with living water from our previous time with God. We argue with the concept of God, but we must wrestle with the presence of God.

They may not admit it or even realize they experience God's love through us in the moment. They may not ever admit it to us. But, they will be curious about this expression of God's love and affection they experienced through our validation of and cooperation with them.

When we seek and find God in that safe and secret place[96] we become filled with everything we need. We become filled to overflowing with rivers of living water when we meet with the Lord.[97] This is how God uses us to refresh others in him.

It only happens as we trust in the Lord fully, and do not rely on our own ability to assess or understand a person or situation.[98]

God loves us. He loves all of us so much he sent Jesus, his son to die for us when we were not walking with him. God is our example to follow. God validated and cooperated with humanity, even when he could not disagree with us more. Incredible!

The Love of the Lord

God loved us and sent his son to die for us when we trusted our own understanding. We accepted the ways of the world while rejecting the ways of God. Yet, God still loved us even when we were in the world. This means we can be sure God loves everyone, whether they are still in the world or not.[99]

When we follow the Lord and someone disagrees with us about anything, it would be easy for us to assume we are right since we walk with the Lord. We could easily conclude the reason they disagree with us is because they do not walk with the Lord.

Or, maybe they just need to grow and mature in the Lord, like we have.

Of course, this would be foolish, not to mention arrogant. If we truly walk with the Lord and in his mighty power, we are able to reach out, care for, love, validate through conversation, and remain in cooperative connection to anyone with whom we have a disagreement.

We do this because our fulfillment does not come from their agreeing with, validating, or cooperating with us. Our fulfillment comes directly from God.

There is no agreement between the mind set on the world and the mind set on the Kingdom of God. God loved us and sent Jesus to rescue us from our sins even when we totally rejected him, mocked him, went our own way away from him, and when we disagreed with him.

This is the perfect picture of ultimate validation and cooperation with someone with whom you do not agree. God did not need us to love, validate, or cooperate with him in order for him to express his love for or to us.

God's unending love is so extensive it moved him to send his son. Jesus loved the Father so much he agreed and came to die for us. As we come to faith in Jesus, the condemnation has been removed. This is what Jesus came to do.[100] How dare we try to put it back on anyone who has come to faith in him?

No Condemnation

If we throw judgment and condemnation on someone, it is a sure sign we moved from the security of the secret place. Perhaps we plain and simply have not met with God in the secret place recently. The strategy for *Outside Words* always has to go back to the solid Foundation of God.

When we are secure in God, we do not need to run down others to try to feel better about ourselves. Nor do we need to try to get affirmation from the outside words of others. When we are secure in God, the only thing that makes us feel better is when we bless other people and use our outside words to build up those around us, rather than tear down anyone.

How can we effectively cooperate with someone by using our outside words? We can acknowledge their thoughts, their feelings, their personhood, and their personal value.

As we interact with their thoughts, we make effort to appreciate their investment in our life by sharing from their heart. Remember, we do not have to affirm or agree with their thoughts, but we can acknowledge their unique perspective and their point of view.

This is different from repeating the information shared with us back to them in different words. We can use more outside words of our own, and validate them again by showing them we acknowledge and honor them, separate from their opinions.

We can cooperate with them like this even when we disagree with them or when we do not want to talk about a particular subject that interests them. Of course, cooperating with a person does not involve having to be a part of inappropriate discussions.

There is a difference between listening to someone about something that does not interest you and enduring an abusive conversation. There may be times to politely excuse yourself from time to time.

Selfless Outside Words

Listen to the following paired examples and see if you can tell a difference from one statement to the next.

"It figures that is what you think. All you want to do is mess up anything that is in order!"

"Though I do not understand completely, it makes sense to me how you can feel that way. God has designed you with such creativity."

The first example is full of reacting with self. It is judgmental, labeling, and full of self-defense and striving at self-validating. The second example is full of validating the other by acknowledging the person, as well as their God given design.

Really, how hard would it be to validate others by seeing them through the lens of God?

Compare the following statements.

"God has given you such a mind for details. It is amazing how God has chosen you to display his characteristic of order to this world. I am grateful for it, because it is an area of lack in my life."

This is so much better than the following.

"Quit nagging about every little thing. Live a little. Must you always be so anal about everything?"

Even when we are in a conversation with someone with whom we disagree and we are pressured to agree with them, we have options. Cooperation that strengthens connection does not mean having to succumb to manipulation.

If we find ourselves in this situation, we can navigate the conversation back to them, rather than their opinion. We tie the conversation back to their existence and who they are. We honor the person, not the topic.

It can frustrate us when we are pressured to either give our opinion on something that we would rather not, or to say whether or not we agree with a person. But, if we have our Foundation in place, we can call out to God for help validating and cooperating with them even as we stand our ground.

It could be that they have never had any idea of God's love for them. It could also be that for the moment, they are distracted from that realization and they are trying to validate themselves through our agreement with them.

This is no different than when we seek validation and cooperation from others rather than from God. When this happens to us, we need to return to a God-centered focus. When we are around others and they experience this, we can help them re-focus on God by identifying their personal qualities as gifts of God as in the example above.

Regardless of how we are treated, whether we are used, neglected, honored, or not honored, we can honor others while pointing them back to their Creator.

Cooperating With God

We must make room for people whether we agree with them, like them, or not. Every person is part of God's plan to bear his image to this world. When we offer validation and cooperation to people who are other than us, different from us, or even annoying to us, we validate and cooperate with God's plan for this world.

The Church misses out on so many incredible people when we turn away by hushing them rather than first validating and cooperating with them. We can celebrate a person's existence and that God created them without agreeing with or promoting things in which we do not believe.

We realize that God created them with specific and unique qualities to offer to this world without agreeing with everything they say, or with every choice they make. No matter what, we must keep talking and connecting. We must keep relating to, validating, and cooperating with others if we are going to strengthen connection or solidify community.

Intimacy with and validation from God in our personal lives helps us avoid the urge to burst out first from our own need for validation. From our outside words with God, we use inviting outside words as we have conversations with others.

This empowers us to avoid dismissive attitudes and bossiness with people. At the same time, we are less likely to try to control the conversation. Instead, we serve the other by leading them in conversation about themselves or their own concerns. We can first be a listening ear for what they have to contribute.

Looking Ahead

Just like the first step, Validation, the second step, Cooperation does not take much time or effort. However, it does need to be a matter of intentionality.

Donation is the third step in *Outside Words*. We will discuss this in the next chapter.

Once we have simplified conversation through Validation and strengthened connection through Cooperation, the time has come to go deeper and build and solidify community as we begin our third step and offer our Donation.

DONATION
SOLIDIFY COMMUNITY
STEP THREE

Each time I experience and survive rejection,
I further overcome being controlled by the fear of it.

Like Jesus Did

Our journey through *Outside Words* is built on the Foundation strategy to seek, find, hear, believe, and repeat God's own outside words. This is modeled in the Bible Jesus' lifestyle. He often took time away from others to invest in time alone with God.

Jesus did this so he could hear God and repeat what he heard from God. We need to practice the same lifestyle. Once we experience God and receive fulfillment as we read the Bible, pray, and through relationship with his Spirit within us, we have something of value to offer to others.

We do so through our own use of outside words as we speak out of the fullness of God overflowing from within.

The first step, Validation taught us the importance of validating the person apart from anything they say or have to offer.

We hear God speak their value as one he created. We extend the same validation.

This can be done by intentionally noticing them and caring for them. Simple conversation about their lives surpasses small talk of things like clothing and the weather, and works wonders in extending compassion.

We continue to acknowledge and validate the value in the other person's worth as a creation of God as we begin the second step, Cooperation. It is here we begin to strengthen connection with this unique person that we are validating.

We cooperate with them as we make space for them to share what is on their minds or what they are feeling.

We continue to honor the person even as we cooperate with their desire to speak and be heard. In this manner we never stop validating the person even when we move on to cooperating with them. Once validation and cooperation are in place, the third step is in order. Now it is time for making our Donation. It is here that we move into solidifying community.

We never stop validating the person even when we move on to cooperating with them. Yet, we, too, have worth and value to add to the conversation and relational connecting. In fact, we are just as valuable as they. All the worth and validation we extend to others can be extended to ourselves, as well. Remember, we have already received it from God.

This is why the Foundation strategy of first spending time with God is so vital. It is here alone we get taught, loved, prophesied over, corrected, healed, validated, and cooperated with by God. We also gain God's Donation, too.

We gain understanding, wisdom, courage, instruction, and everything else we need from God.

Like Jesus, we must get filled up from God before we can overflow his goodness, validation, and cooperation to any other person, or have a donation worth giving.

Rightly Relating to God and to Others

When we validate others, we do not lose our own validation. Instead, when we value and honor others by making room for them to share their opinion, we reinforce the validation we received from God rather than losing it.

As we give consideration to others, we give out what we received from our relationship with God. The same is true for honor. I do not give others my honor and am left without any honor. Rather, I give honor out of the honor that I receive from God.

It is important to really grasp this. When we use our outside words, we do not practice people pleasing mindsets where we become too focused on or absorbed in others. Neither do we enter into addiction mindset where it is all about us. Instead, we rightly relate to God, which enables us to relate in healthy ways to ourselves and to others.

Take a short break in the reading to refer back to the paired comments in the last chapter.

It is possible for someone God designed who is more ordered to bless those in his or her life who are challenged with order. Likewise, a person who is more inclined toward randomness can also bless those in their lives who prefer to live and work more orderly.

It is not about only one person in the conversation receiving the blessings of validation, and cooperation. But it is about first validating and cooperating with the other party before offering something to be heard by making a Donation one's own thoughts and feelings.

As a result of the Foundation strategy of spending more time with God and being validated by his outside words to us, we are more able to and likely to offer validating outside words to others.

Even as we validate other people and recognize personal worth placed on them by God, we reinforce our own personal validation knowing that we are just as valuable.

Giving Honor to God

Let me reemphasize, when we honor others by making space for the thoughts and opinions of others, we do not just honoring the person by operating out of the honor that God has given us. We also reinforce our God-given honor.

It is really not a matter of who gets honor and who does not. Rather, it is about honoring God while we honor the people Jesus honored when he died on the cross for them.

We do not lose honor or validation when we give out of it. The more we invest to seek and find God, the more help we have to empower us though the day. We have more simple courtesies to extend to other people, as well.

When we operate out of God's fulfillment, we are more aware of and better able to attend to those around us. We have godly intentions. We are better leaders because we lead people to God so they can be filled by God, rather than bringing them to ourselves to try to get them to fill us.

Hearing from God better enables us to love, honor, and respect the people we talk to even when we disagree with them. This applies to all conversations, regardless of relational dynamics of those involved.

Whether it is friends talking, a conversation between a parent and a child, or a meeting between leaders and employees or volunteers they serve. *Outside Words* can be used in any setting personal or public, small or large.

God chose to create us and he chose to design us each in the way he did for a purpose. If we believe God created the other person or people, we also must validate how God created them to be, to grow, to explore, to mature, to come to know, and to be transformed by him. In doing so, we honor God.

Remember, in do not validate a person's opinions, beliefs, or decisions, rather we are validate God.

Free From Expectations

It is a matter of our expectations. If we enter any conversation and expect others to use the strategies and steps of outside words to make room for our outside words, we can easily be disappointed and even become judgmental.

However if we employ the strategies and steps of *Outside Words*, we have already received fulfillment from God and will not seek it from another.

Personally, I find it is so freeing to enter a conversation from a place where I do not need to be understood or agreed with because I have come from a place of already being heard and understood by God.

Even when God disagrees with me, he still understands and validates me. God never rejects me but continues to draw me toward him and his ways. Rather than reject people, we can continually draw them toward God and his ways.

Covey taught us to seek first to understand the other person, then to seek to be understood. [101] I propose that we back up just a bit by seeking the Lord first. From this place of being heard and validated we then seek to validate, cooperate with, and donate to others with whom we converse.

I am convinced that fulfillment from God is the best place to begin. From there, it will not threaten us if others do not want to know who we are, or if they do not invest the time to get to know us. It may be painful, though.

It is natural to want mutually validating, cooperating, and donating conversation, connection and community. However, not everyone is able to or willing to put the effort to engage in this manner. Nor is will every conversation be with someone who has interest to listen to or acknowledge our worth or Donation to the conversation.

Vulnerable Risks

Validation, Cooperation and Donation are steps I continue to learn as the Lord teaches and stretches me. I gain understanding from God that helps me see problem spots in my life and seek further guidance. I confess, repent, and ask for God's help. Thankfully, it is not always correction that I hear.

In fact, God also speaks encouraging and empowering words to me during my personal conversation with God, as well as through the Bible. He challenges me to believe the good things he says about me. Dare I believe what God has told me? Dare I move in the directions he calls me to? Why wouldn't I?

When I make a Donation in interpersonal conversation from my own thoughts and feelings, I become vulnerable and risk being rejected. But, this is a risk that must be taken. Being fearful of risk is wasteful and squandering. It never leads to success.

Think about it. It has been said that rejection equals success.[102]This means that those who run from rejection run from success.[103]

This is also true of relating and conversing. Those who run from rejection in communication run from successful conversation, connection and community. There is nothing of value that does not involve risk. Just ask the servant who squandered opportunity because he was too afraid to risk.[104]

When we extend value to others, we risk rejection. Maybe others are not able to receive, or they may refuse to be receptive in that moment. There is no way to avoid the risk that is involved when we seek to benefit, build up, and bless others.

Lack of opportunity to make our donation is another risk we face. When we let others speak first, we risk not being able to share what we have to say due to time constraints, interruptions, or for other reasons.

Perhaps the greatest risk involved in step three, Donation, is when we open our hearts and authentically share our thoughts and feelings. Will we be rejected? Will anyone still be interested in listening by the time it gets to our turn to talk?

However, these risks must be taken. The risk to cooperate by letting others go first will then be followed with the risk of offering a self-disclosing Donation.

We must use our own outside words not just to bless other people with Validation and Cooperation. If we do not offer our Donation, it will lead to lopsided discussion that overlooks the value God has given to one or more involved in the conversation, namely ourselves.

It is imperative that when we do so, we make a Donation of our thoughts and feelings, that is, a donation from our whole heart.

Free From Codependency

Personally, I deal with the codependent temptation to not bother making donations, that is, to not share my thoughts and feelings. This is typically true in conversation where there is no validation from the other party. It is especially true when there is insult, aggression, or disregard from the other person.

However, I train myself to step out and speak up. This is not from a need to be heard. My need to be heard has already been fulfilled by God. Rather, it is from the place of acknowledgment that what God has given me to donate to the conversation is worth the risk of being rejected.

When I have to use great force to make a space for my Donation in a conversation, it often does not seem worth it. The truth is that we all do have value, whether others choose to recognize it or not, whether others choose to make space for us or not. My Donation is just as valuable as someone else's. So is yours.

One of the unhealthy methods I learned and previously operated in was to self-protect by keeping my thoughts and feelings to myself. As a result, I rarely voiced disagreement (especially with those who have not learned how to be okay with differing opinions).

In addition, I chose the less hectic route of just going along with those who try to be in control of every conversation or situation. I did not want to fight the battle to try to be included or heard.

Now, a pattern of risk based relating in my life has developed. Fear had to be broken down by the transforming grace of God. I realize that most who usually dominate conversations without making room for others are just striving to get the validation from people that they have yet to get from God.

No longer do I have to keep my thoughts and feelings in line with someone else's. In Christ, I am free to be how he created me. Free to exist and glorify God how he designed me to. In Christ, I am also free to make an authentic Donation regardless of the other person's state of being.

It is not up to other's moods or whims to determine how I relate.

By God's transformational grace, I experience liberty. I no longer enable controlling addictive behavior in others, or code-pendent self-protecting temptations in myself like I used to. The change has come as God empowers me to put forth effort to use my outside words more in conversation, connection, and community.

Learning From My Mistakes

Refraining from making donations in the past just to keep things simple was a mistake that I had to realize and overcome by God's guidance and grace. The assuredness and validation I received from God made it possible.

The other person's level of extending validation or cooperation (or lack of extending the same) in a conversation must not set the pace for me. I must honor God and enter into even the most one-sided conversations to make the Donation of thoughts and feelings (from my heart) God has given me to extend to others.

To welcome, make room for, and receive my thoughts and feelings are up to those with whom I speak. It is not my responsibility to try to make someone hear me.

Healthy relating is better than just going along with others. I so much more enjoy validating others while continuing to walk in the validation I received from God. As called for, I can now experience God's peace while validating, cooperating with, and offering donations even while in settings with those who do not receive me.

As I learn to experience more of God, I grow in faith and courage. I learn to better validate others, as well as myself. I not only validate how God wants to work his purposes through how he created others, I also validate how God wants to work his purposes in how he created me.

"Risk-lationship"©

You have value to add, and so do I. That is why the *Outside Words* basics of putting forth the effort to actually use more spoken words to state and clarify what I want to communicate is so important.

It is vital, to take a chance in what I call "risk-lationship"© and risk rejection in an effort to engage in authentic conversation, connection, and community with others.[105]

As I do risk-relating in healthy ways, I acknowledge that God created me to be, and who God created me to be. God is validated as I repeat his outside words to me. I intentionally take what God has given to me, engage it, and surrender it back to God so that he can shape it into what he wants me to donate.

Then, when God has readied it and readied me, he brings it forward in perfect timing. This changes me. It changes the patterns in my brain. As this happens, I get transformed by renewing my mind toward the ways of God.[106]

You have value to add and I have value to add.

When we come to this third step, Donation, there are things to consider. We cannot make people listen to us. It is impossible to force a person to validate us or recognize and engage with our value. Chances are you have already learned this from your own life experience.

I learned this in each of the two painful relationship struggles mentioned earlier. Only when both parties surrender to the Lord and become willing to humble themselves before the Lord will there be any chance or hope of healthy healing and continued wellness in a relationship.

In no way did I feel like humbling myself to the Lord in regard to either of these relationship struggles. I felt too exposed, too vulnerable. Besides, I thought I was right, and I also believed I was wronged.

It was painful to back down and give up my right to self-protect. This was especially painful in the relationship where the other person continued to gear up and voice their argument about how right they were and how wrong I was.

I had to desperately ask God to help me humble myself before the Lord because there was no way that I could do it on my own.

No Guarantee

In the relationship where there has been much healing, God did empower me to humble myself before him. The other person humbled themselves before God, as well. Over time, God has worked wonders in that relationship and continues to do so today.

The other relationship is moving forward, but is still a work that needs progress. I am convinced God will work wonders in this relationship, too. But a process it is.

Though this is not my preference, it is my prayer request that God will empower me to walk the journey and validate this person (innate value given by God), cooperate with them (whether or not I agree with them), and donate to them (whether or not they accept me or my donation).

I will enter into this risk-lationship by taking the risk to bring more of my outside words into the picture. Even as I step forward and engage with more outside words, I am not guaranteed the others I talk with will choose to or be able to respond to me. Neither is there guarantee they will choose to, or even be able to receive the validation I extend.

Facing this helps me realize how vital the Foundation strategy is. I simply must spend personal time with God each day. It is important to remember I am not to try to force anyone to engage with me in any certain way, or engage with me at all. None of us should do this.

Using our outside words to validate others does not guarantee they will accept validation from us or accept us. This is why throughout the day we must be fulfilled with God's outside words to us and become familiar with God's outside words about others.

Other's response to us neither validates nor invalidates us or our outside words. Other's rejection of our outside words does not disqualify what we have spoken.

Power to bless was released as the words were spoken. The other person may not have received it, but we can still experience the power of speaking words that benefit, build up, and bless over others with our outside words.

In the same manner, if they reject not only our words, but our person as well, we still do not have to worry about being rejected. We have already received full acceptance from our time with God. The same is true for us as we make our donation.

When we are fulfilled in God, we do not need to be received by others, be agreed with, or be received from.

After all, when a person rejects or deflects our compliments and validations, it can make us hesitant to make ourselves vulnerable again to offer a donation of our own personal thoughts and feelings from our hearts.

This common fear can be overcome as we admit it and then rehearse in our minds God's already spoken outside words of acceptance over us.

Speaking the Truth

We also rehearse God's outside words about this person. God fully loves them and calls them to himself. The more we respond to rejection with God's words, the more God's outside words will wash over us. This equips us to remember and repeat God's words.

God's loving acceptance (of ourselves, as well as of those with whom we are speaking) overrules the most painful rejection from other people every time. The pain may linger, but in light of God's love and acceptance, it lessens as it heals.

I am convinced God's love brought Christ through what he suffered for me.

I continue to learn rejection is no longer something to fear or avoid. Instead, it is just be par for the course. The more I risk authentic vulnerable relationship with others, the more I experience rejection. Each time I experience and survive rejection, I further overcome being controlled by the fear of it.[107]

Not everyone has developed their capacity to accept validation, cooperation, or a donation from another person. Not everyone will accept me. That is okay. It is not only okay, it is actually good. Rejection from people helps me return to and rely on God as my Foundation source of acceptance.

No longer do the labels other people try to hang on me matter. I may learn from what others say, but the final say is from God. This applies to us all.

Likewise, when we use outside words, we must not look for ways to label other people. In fact, we must make great effort to not make a donation of a label to another person. Even when we recognize characteristics of people, we are not to lock them into stereotypes.

We have to get over our own fears and not freeze people into what we remember them to be, where we want them to be, or where we think they are.[108] Otherwise, we try to relate to them as the label, rather than relate to the unique, individual, and valuable person they are.

Look past the labels (even their own self-labels) and love them truthfully. Talk to them about what is going on in their lives. Find out what is important to them. Enter into risk-lationship © with them where they are. You may be surprised at who they really are.

As we donate value while communicating, it is not to fix, control, or manipulate the person or the conversation. Rather, it is to glorify God as we agree with him that this person has value because he created them with worth.

Likewise, we each have value to add and will do so as we engage and offer of ourselves *to* God *for* others.[109]

It is important to note that we also must not receive labels people give us. It is useless to try to live out what we have been labeled. Only God knows and can give us understanding of our true identity.

Coaching Questions: What About You?

Pray this prayer before you begin.

> God, you know what you have given me to give back to the world - this insight, this encouragement, this love, this acceptance, this truth. It is your value that you gave to me and I must not keep it to myself. I experience it, engage with it, and I must donate it. I must express it in my outside words. I must enter into risk-lationship© and offer myself more while making more room for others. Thanks for your help, God. Amen.

Think of a relationship in which you struggle at least a little. Ask yourself the following questions and take the time to answer them.

What are the best outside words for me to use in this relational struggle?

_____
_____
_____
_____
_____

What do I need to share with this particular person?

_____
_____
_____
_____
_____

How do I need to speak these things to them?

_____
_____
_____
_____
_____

If you have not completed this exercise, please do so before you continue reading and taking notes.

Giving God

Over the years, I have gotten pretty good at bouncing back and either pressing on through or past rejection. Of course, sometimes with rejection comes labeling from others. In such cases, the rejection from others needs to be responded to. I validate them as people while I reject their labels. To resist a label is not to reject the one who does the labeling.

God chose to draw us to him and to use us to express himself to others. What better reason to solidify community with someone than to bear God's image to them. Not one of our mistakes or failures is enough to disqualify us from being called to God and to walk in God's ways.

None of the wounds I experienced, or any of the wounds I inflicted onto others or myself can invalidate God's purposes, plans, and will for my life or theirs. Neither can any wound from another keep me from drawing near to God.

The same is true for you and for everyone. This is really good news because chances are we have all been wounded and we all have wounded others.

The things that we have learned do not change God's plans. Likewise, the things that we have yet to learn do not change God's plans.

We must learn to trust that God validates us. God honors where we are and will use us from our current life situation as we keep relating with him and also with other people.

Learning From Others

Part of what I disagree with in another person may be what God uses to teach me something, and vice versa. Our differences are not to our detriment, but rather to our benefit.

What you have to donate to a conversation matters. It is important. It is valuable to authentic relating, which cannot happen unless your inside words appropriately become your outside words.

If people accept and engage in our personal donation, that is wonderful. Then the cycle of validating, cooperating, and donating back and forth can go on as long as both parties care to continue. If they do not accept, engage, or make room for our value to be added, then we can still be secure in God.

In addition, we can be sure that our goal of using outside words to benefit, build up, and bless as we bear God's image to them has still been accomplished. God has blessed us, and walked in God's ways as we loved and respected others from God's heart.

Donation involves giving to others what God has given to us to give to others. When we offer it, we cannot force someone else to receive it. We cannot force anyone to believe it. But we can still offer it.

We must offer to others the validation we have received from God. Even God does not force anyone to receive from him. Just like the first two steps, Validation and Cooperation, this third step, Donation calls for walking in humility.

We must humble ourselves before the Lord in order to receive from him both what we need for ourselves, as well as what we need to donate to meet the needs of others. There is no way to donate things of God without first having received God's donation to us.

Looking Ahead

The next chapter will provide an explanation of Filtration, the final strategy of *Outside Words*. This biblical principle is the complimentary bookend to the Foundation strategy of first spending time with God. Just as we must begin with God, we must also end with God.

FILTRATION
THE ENDING WITH GOD STRATEGY

Continue to learn from person to person
what is considered a blessing
and what does not bless them.

Filtration

S trategization. There's that word again. In the Foundation
chapter, we began learning the process of *Outside Words*
as we explored the first strategy. Foundation prepared us
to simplify conversation, solidify connection, and strengthen
community through the use of *Outside Words*.

This second strategy, Filtration will teach us the much needed
skill of editing how we outwardly express the thoughts and feelings of our hearts.

Even at this point in the process, it is vital to keep reminding
ourselves what using *Outside Words* entails. The basics of *Outside
Words* simply calls for the use of more outwardly expressed communication with spoken words, signs, symbols, or any other form
of outward expression. Once the basics are understood, we must
prepare by moving into the strategies.

Foundation, the first strategy, taught us to seek and find
God, and then to listen for and listen to God's outside words.
This happens as we read the Bible, as well as through personal
witness of the Holy Spirit within the believer.

As we spend time in God's presence and goodness we become more like him and develop God's interest in and God's compassion for other people. This in itself is enough to Validate them (step one) simply for being created by God.

Then, while we continue to validate their personhood, we begin to Cooperate with them (step two) as we listen to them share their thoughts and feelings. Finally, we Donate (step three) our value to the conversation.

Filtration, the second strategy is exactly what it sounds like. We must channel our outside words through the filter of Christ. Just as sure as this process needs to begin with the Foundation strategy, it must also continue with the mindset of God through Filtration.

Your Choice

The reason for this is clear. As we use our outside words for the Lord, we are empowered to stop using them for evil purposes. With every outward communication we make, we can choose to partner in the goodness of the Light or we can choose to partner with the evil of the darkness. We build up or tear down. There is no other choice.

Everything we communicate, whether negatively (with the voice, the inclination of the voice, a raised eyebrow, a hand held up to someone as they try to speak to us...), or positively (arms open wide, leaning toward them as we listen to them, smiling, excited expressions...); every outside word we communicate is either shining God's light into a situation or closing it off with darkness.

The purpose for bookending the three steps of *Outside Words* with this two part strategy process of Foundation and Filtration is that through this we gain God's understanding. Once we have God's understanding, then God becomes our editor. Our very Foundation (God) becomes our Filtration.

This will empower us to speak incredibly amazing things that allow us to edify and solidify relationships. We must be careful to not run past God's Filtration or we will end up using our outside words to tear down rather than benefit, build up, and bless.

Humor

For example, humor. Submitted to the Lord, humor is amazingly beneficial. The Bible teaches us that to be merry is good for us. It is medicine for our souls. When both the emotions and the mind (the whole heart) are merry, it is like the cure we get from medicine.[110]

However, this verse goes on to teach that a broken spirit is in contradiction to being merry. In fact, when a person's spirit is broken, it will result in the drying up of the well spring of their very self.

> Luke 6:45
> *A good man brings good things out of the good stored up in his heart, and an evil man brings evil things out of the evil stored up in his heart. For out of the overflow of his heart his mouth speaks.*

> Proverbs 4:23
> *Above all else, guard your heart, for it is the wellspring of life.*

I recently heard something I used to say to others. It was a simple comment purposed to make a joke of someone in order to get a response of laughter. The man who recently had surgery near his eye was asked if his face still hurt. He answered, "No.". Encouraged by the other man's concern he believed he was being genuinely cared for.

He opened up and began by sharing his experience when suddenly, the first man abruptly cut him off with the age-old sarcastic remark, "Well, your face hurts me." This was followed by some faint nervous and awkward laughing as the rest of the group tried to bring common courtesy back to the conversation.

When humor is used to tear down (curse) rather than to build up (bless), it destroys. Even a simple situation like the one above, humor should not be used to hurt others. Regardless of the laughter that may result from such careless banter, we can be sure that when a person's spirit has been hurt through course or careless joking, damage has been done.

Those being talked to or talked about, as well as those who listen are being negatively affected.[111] We must learn to guard our mouths so that we do not sin by what we say.[112] The only way to do this is to guard the thoughts and feelings of our hearts.

Ephesians chapter five calls such conversing out of place for those who follow Christ.[113] We must choose this day and every day who we will serve with our outside words.

Cut it Out

When we turn light-hearted fun and funny situations into blaming, shaming cut down fights, or word games where we mock others and tear them to pieces (often to their faces), we belittle people and have fun at their expense. This is more costly than any pay off of laughter that may result or any false sense of building-up our self.

In the book of Matthew we learn that with every spoken word or gesture of our outside words we express toward anyone it is as if we are doing the same thing to Jesus, our King.[114]

When God, our Foundation is also the one in charge of our Filtration, we will not curse anyone, not even ourselves with our outside words. Rather we will always bless. God highly regards every person declaring our value by the price Jesus paid on the cross for us.

How dare we devalue God by devaluing and cutting down the very ones God declared worthy?

In 1 Thessalonians 2, Paul assures the church of Thessalonica of his strong desire and previous attempts to come to them. From verse eighteen in the King James Version, we learn that Paul would have already arrived if it were not for the devil's hindrance.

The word translated as "hindrance" in this passage is the Greek word *egkopto*. It is pronounced /eng-kop'-to/. It means to cut into (figuratively), that is to impede, detain, hinder, or to be tedious to.

In part, it is from a word that means to chop, beat the breast in grief, cut down, lament, mourn, or bewail. This also can refer to trying to trip up an opponent in order to win an athletic contest. This word entails the activity of cutting or bumping into, as well as the painful loss and other consequences of such actions.

The hindering activity of the devil described in this passage can be used as an illustration to describe what happens when the members of the Body of Christ cut into one another. There is damage done when the Body of Christ hinders one another through cut downs and other such insults and put downs even if they are done in the name of love, bonding, or just having fun.

Abusing the Bride

When anyone in the Body of Christ, which is also known as the Bride of Christ, cuts down others, they hurt them and hinder them from running their race well. This amounts to the Bride of Christ sabotaging herself through self-injury.

When we cut down one another, we cut into other members of the same body. Though we may win the cut down fight, no one really wins. It is horrific to think of abusing the Bride of Christ, yet we often do.

The Church, Christ's Bride, is not to behave like a self-injuring cutter. Yet that is what we do when we engage in such abrasive attitudes, actions, and verbal assaults. Collectively, we have the self inflicted wounds to prove it.

It is time for the Church to become a safe place, free from damaging activities such as cut downs that cut deep wounds and leave visible scars. We desperately need to grow in our security through our Foundation time with God so that we can benefit, build-up, and bless.

Cutting down or into one another in the Body is self injury that is often cloaked in a false sense of bonding. When one hinders or injures them self, there is disconnect at the deepest level. Even when such activity is highly functional, it does not amount to authentic bonding.

Jesus prayed that we would be one. The church needs to be unified, not divisive in the name of love. It confuses those who truly seek the God of love when we speak of our love for them in one breath, while we hide behind passive aggression and cut them down with the next.

The days ahead for the church will require a connected Body that works well together without deadly friendly fire. One in which the members are filled to overflowing with living water and are able to enjoy and excel in simple conversation that strengthens connection and solidifies community rather than preventing or destroying it.

If we must cut anything, may we learn to cut covenant with one another and enter into self-less uplifting of others as we each humble ourselves, and risk all that we are for the purposes of God on the earth.

Breaking Old Habits

Some of the old habits must be broken if we are to grow up and mature. Healthy relational patterns will develop when our old ways of conversing experience much needed Filtration as we submit them to the Foundation of the love of God.

We can expect our cut down fights to turn into truly creative, humorous, and edifying exchanges that simplify conversation, strengthen connection, and solidify community. Imagine the power of God's light rather than the darkness of the enemy as we engage in competitions of humorous storytelling and hurling blessings rather than insults.

The more secure we become in Christ, the less we will be concerned about others being built up higher than us. We will be free enough to exchange past patterns of harshness for refreshing practices of honor. It is so powerful to uplift someone through speaking blessings to them rather than crushing them down just to get a laugh or try to build ourselves up or self-protect.

Self Examination

Here are some things to consider in order to find out how much Filtration you need to put in place in your conversations.

Do you find yourself able to receive compliments?

If you are not able to receive validation from others' words to you, there is a greater chance you are seek self-validation through your words to others. Ouch! I can relate to this. Can you? If so, it is time to ditch the false humility and embrace the truth of the wonder in which you were created!

Answer these questions to see if this applies to you.

- Do you find yourself starting or engaging in cut down competitions?
- Are your gatherings of family, friends, co-workers, or teammates uplifting and edifying?
- Are they harsh and based on insults, even if in the name of having fun?
- Do you ever try to justify your harsh comments by calling others a baby or a wimp after they have shared with you that your outside words have wounded them?
- Do you find yourself telling others they are too sensitive?
- Do you hear yourself try to justify your cruel outside words by saying you were only joking?

Proverbs 26:18-19
Like a maniac shooting firebands or deadly arrows is one who deceives his neighbor and says, "I was only joking!

Again, ouch!

Confession

I remember decades ago when I first learned the importance of word choice and the power of words. Some friends were over for a night of conversation, connection, and community. We were just hanging out, eating, playing games, talking and having a "fun" evening.

Unfortunately, this rarely involved anything uplifting and usually involved harassing each other and cutting down one another in front of the group.

One brave friend spoke up about the harshness of the so called fun. Her honest vulnerability was an affront to my insecure self-protecting "funny" insults.

The choices before me were to validate and cooperate with her and offer an edifying donation of an appropriate amends, or to dismiss her further and use her as a target to try to defend my immature behavior.

Rather than donate a heartfelt apology to the conversation, I did something I lived to regret. I further invalidated my friend while striving to excuse and validate myself. I actually told her she should know by now that when she came over she needed to check her feelings at the door.

Of course, as everyone resounded with laughter. I used their response to try to justify my own destructive outside words. I did this rather than face the truth that I was using her to try to gain something for myself.

How cruel and foolish this was of me. How blinded I was to do this all in the name of having fun. I was clueless and heartless. Even though I was unaware of it at the time, I was desperate for both the Foundation and the Filtration of God, to be sure.

Coaching Questions: What About You?

Have you ever tried to build yourself up by tearing down others? If so, what happened? How did it really make you feel?

_____
_____
_____
_____
_____

Has anyone ever tried to build themselves up by tearing down you or your opinion? If so, what was that experience like?

_____
_____
_____
_____
_____

What can you learn about yourself and your need for God from this exercise?

_____
_____
_____
_____
_____

Did you find relationships in your life where you could use some of Filtration on your outside words?
If so, list a few of them here.

1. _____
_____

2. _____
_____

3. _____

   _____

Most likely you did. If you did not, you can check with those closest to you. Just ask your spouse, children, parents, employees, teammates, friends, and co-workers. They may be able to fill you in, and it may surprise you.

Practice

Here is an excellent way to practice the Filtration of your outside words.

Watch and allow yourself to honestly respond to a news program, video, or commercial of some sort. This way, you can be honest and real while learning about yourself without hurting or crushing someone else.

Are your thoughts and feelings good or overly critical toward the people and the work you see?

This may surprise you. It also may reflect whether the thoughts and feelings that come from your heart and out of your mouth in the course of your day are typically positive or negative.

In the areas that you are negative, ask God what is behind your negativity?

The more that we refer back to the Foundation strategy of being with and learning from God, the more we will be secure in him and overflow with God's blessings for others. Our outside words always need to bless those we talk to and benefit others who hear us, as well.

Think about it. When we are cruel and harsh with someone, invalidating them by not making room for their voice, or by making fun of them, then we are not just hurting them. We are hurt others, as well. The image we bear to them is not that of God, the one image we were created to bear.

Lesson Learned

Decades ago, while working at the post office, I was boxing mail on the wall. That is, I was putting letters, magazines, and such into the appropriate post office boxes rented by individuals and businesses.

It was not unusual for most of the employees on our shift to wind up boxing mail on the wall to ensure on time delivery. As we worked boxing mail, we often shared casual conversation.

I remember one day on the wall in particular because it marked the beginning of a life-long change in me. As usual, I joked and laughed with other employees as I tried to speak the biggest smart aleck remark or cut down. One man gently, yet powerfully came up to me privately and asked me why I was so cynical.

Of course, I denied it and tried to excuse it. I said, "I am not cynical. I am funny!"

Defensively, I thought to myself, "Who does he think he is, this kill-joy, to accuse me like that?" But the sinking feeling in my gut would not let me get out of answering his piercing and nagging question.

Why was I so cynical? And, how could I honestly excuse my aggressive attitude and disrespectful behavior as being a blessing and having fun?

This was the day I began to really learn the importance of other people. It was also when God began to teach me to surrender humor, as well as every other part of my existence to him. If what I am using humor for is not validating people or God, their Creator, then I am misusing the gift of humor.

I cannot use enough outside words to express my gratitude to God for changing the way I see, regard, and treat the dear people that he has put in my life to express his love to. I am still in the learning process and suspect that it will need to continue as long as I live. Even so, some transformation so far in the process evokes gratitude within.

Progress, Not Perfection

Recently, I was at a car dealership having to barter over the price to be paid for thousands of dollars of unauthorized repairs that were done to my car. I did not know about the extra repairs until I went to pick up the car.

Since these were not agreed upon repairs, we had to negotiate a settlement. As you can imagine, the discussion became pretty intense as the manager insisted that I pay for all of the repairs.

This was years ago as the concept of *Outside Words* was just beginning to form in my mind.

Rather than my usual response to the louder, more demanding, and more controlling a person became (pull away from the situation), I began to intentionally use my outside words (lean into the situation). Since I was reassured of my secure Foundation in the Lord that day, I was able to trust God's lead in that conversation.

I did not have to analyze on my own what I should say or not say. Instead, I could simply hear and follow the Lord's lead in the moment.

God taught me much that day. I learned about stepping out with confidence in him, and to not defend myself by yelling back. I learned to use my outside words to stand up to someone who was trying to use their louder voice and misuse their position of authority over the shop while posturing their bigger body in such a way as to bully me and try to intimidate me.

By God's Foundation of grace I was able to have this conversation without using putdowns, even while deflecting putdowns hurled my way. This was not my historical mode of operation, though it is becoming more so as time goes by.

I learned that each conversation can teach me much. This one taught me that I needed to learn how to add more things into the mix like patience, kindness, and mercy rather than just not speaking put downs while refusing to back down from this type of situation.

It is likely that I will not have to face such a conversation again, because another thing I learned was to use even more outside words, both spoken and written, in contracting conversations in the future!

New Tools

However, if the event arises that I am in such a conversation again, I have the *Outside Words* dual strategy process of Foundation and Filtration to utilize. Also available are the three steps of Validation, Cooperation, and Donation.

I can invest in validating the other person. I can invest in cooperating with them by listening and hearing them, then donating in respectful ways even if thousands of dollars are at stake!

There is such freedom in this process of *Outside Words*. My relating through conversation, connection, and community are better than they have ever been. I and others are grateful.

It is not unusual for me to hear, in the moment, the critique of the Lord. When I listen to his outside words, I make adjustments along the way even as he guides.

Or, if I am stubborn during the conversation, I will most likely deflect God's voice in the moment. In this case, I hear God's conviction later and hopefully make the corrections I need to, such as offering the appropriate amends. Even forgiving in the moment can be quicker than I previously realized.

Pastor Kris Vallotton of Bethel Church in Redding, California relates an experience where he was able to receive insight from his personal assistant when she shared with him that his outside words sometimes hurt others' feelings. To this Vallotton replied, "I thought I was being funny, but apparently I had actually made her my latest victim."

Though this pastor apologized, it was not until God showed him that he realized the problem was not another person being overly sensitive. Rather, the problem had to do with work that needed to be done within his own heart.[115]

The practice of *Outside Words* is a process. Do not do the steps without first making sure your Foundation and Filtration are in place. Remember, laughter is not the filter, God is. Though harshness and course joking can be funny and cause laughter, it is only through uplifting that a heart will be truly merry.

Season of Surrender

Last year, God called me to invest extra time with him daily for a period of ninety days. This took some steps of faith and some rearranging of my schedule and my plans. I could not have guessed what this would be like before I engaged God at this level.

Experiencing God at this depth brought about an intense season of surrender and repentance.

I could not get closer to God without spending more time with him. I could not spend more time with God without him showing me about himself, as well as what he was showing me about myself.

He is the Light and he lit up things in my life that I had to either deal with or try to go into denial about.

Ninety days of being with God led to and empowered much confession, repentance, and surrender. I began to wonder if there was anything left the same about me or my belief in him as it was when this process began.

I experienced so many wonderful things in the Lord as I turned toward him. God continually showed me his love and his will for me, as well as my errors and misunderstandings. He empowered me to receive his love at a new level, take new steps of faith, and correct behaviors, mind sets, attitudes, and so much more.

Near the end of the ninety days, I asked God what was next after this season of surrender. His outside words to me assured me that this was not a season. This is how I was to live my life. This is what following Christ looks like.

God began to speak to my heart and show me how much time I spent with him and the consequences of the sacrifice of personal and social time. He showed me how much more I now use my outside words with him, and the increase in the amount of his outside words that I can now hear.

God showed me what has happened in our relationship as well as in so many different aspects of my life. This is now a lifestyle of getting closer to God, repenting from my old ways of thinking, and surrendering my all for God's Kingdom purposes and mindset.

It is about enhancing my relationship with God so that I can be used in validating other people and cooperating with them while donating the value that God has given me.

Paul's Outside Words to Us

The beginning of Ephesians 4 has to do with the Foundation strategy of seeking God and being shaped into his image. As we grow and mature in God, we experience more of his influence in our lives. This results in our outside words becoming a clearer reflector of God's own outside words through his process of Filtration.

Please give some time to meditate on and ponder the following verses.

Ephesians 4:14-15

Then we will no longer be infants, tossed back and forth by the waves, and blown here and there by every wind of teaching and by the cunning and craftiness of people in their deceitful scheming. Instead, speaking the truth in love, we will in all things grow up into him who is the head, that is Christ.

Ephesians 4:21-24

You, however did not come to know Christ in that way. Surely you heard of him and were taught in him in accordance with the truth that is in Jesus. You were taught, with regard to your former way of life, to put off your old self, which is being corrupted by its deceitful desire, to be made new in the attitude of your minds; and to put on the new self, created to be like God in true righteousness and holiness.

The closer we get to God the more we will walk out our faith on the Foundation of who he is. We will be more ready to present God and bring him into our conversations. The next verses exemplify how God, the Foundation, is also the Filtration.

Ephesians 4:29-30
Do not let any unwholesome talk come out of your mouths, but only what is helpful for building others up according to their needs, that it may benefit those who listen. And do not grieve the Holy Spirit of God, with whom you were sealed for the day of redemption.

Ephesians 5:1-4
Follow God's example, therefore, as dearly loved children and walk in the way of love, just as Christ loved us and gave himself up for us as a fragrant offering and sacrifice to God.

But among you there must not be even a hint of sexual immorality, or of any kind of impurity, or of greed, because these are improper for God's holy people. Nor should there be any obscenity, foolish talk or course joking, which are out of place, but rather thanksgiving.

Ephesians 5:15-20
Be very careful, then, how you live — not as unwise, but as wise, making the most of every opportunity, because the days are evil. Therefore, do not be foolish, but understand what the Lord's will is. Do not get drunk on wine, which leads to debauchery. Instead, be filled with the Spirit. Speak to one another with psalms, hymns, and spiritual songs. Sing and make music from your heart to the Lord, always giving thanks to God the Father for everything, in the name of our Lord, Jesus Christ.

We have to build on the Foundation of the Holy Spirit of God. We must choose which spirit we will listen to. Will we be drunk on wine and be led to debauchery, or will we be filled with the Spirit of God? We each must choose if we will listen to the spirit of God or if we will listen to the spirit of the age.

This whole section of Ephesians talks about outside words. It also teaches about outside actions and outside attitudes as well. All of our attitudes, actions, and words come from what is in our hearts (our thoughts and feelings).

We must spend time with God if we are to take on his character. We must find that safe secret place, that refuge that we can pull away, to experience God, and be blessed so we can bless others.[116]

Daily Filtration

When we have the Filtration of God we generally know what to do and what not to do. We can know what to say, how to say it, why to say it, and when to say it. When we surrender to God, our Foundation, we are connected to his Filtration as well, since they are one in the same.

So, when you speak to someone and you feel like your eyes are about to roll upward, or you are about to laugh at or mock someone (who bears God's image) rather than bless them, just take a breath and call out to God to help you. "Lord, Jesus Christ! Help me!"

Instead of repeating non-blessings (curses) we have heard spoken to us or to other people, what we need to do is default to thanksgiving.

Are you tempted to cut someone down? Default to thanksgiving.

Do you have a knee-jerk reaction to spew out a sarcastic remark in the name of Christian fellowship? Default to thanksgiving.

Start by adding thanksgiving and gratitude. Begin with internal mini retreats back to the Lord throughout the day. From there begin anew each time. From there hear the Lord afresh. Listen to God's outside words and repeat them. Hear him again, and go tell other people what you heard.

Go back to your Foundation as many times as you can during the day. Strap on your Filtration in the morning strap it back on again each time it comes off during the day.

When I cooperate with a person and make room for their words which happen to be uncaring or even damaging, then I get to learn a little bit more about how God loved me even when I caused pain.

When I honor someone as they speak words I disagree with, I can gain a deeper understanding of God's unconditional love he expressed to me. God expressed his unconditional love to me so that I can receive it, experience it, and also extend it to others.

Worth the Effort

Out of the two relationships where I struggled with communication which I mentioned earlier, the struggle communicating in one began years ago. However, this struggle has ended because of the decisions we each made and continue to make to recognize each other as both equal and valuable according to God.

We each also incorporated room in our conversations for outside words both from each other as well as to each other. This co-effort to simplify conversation has definitely strengthened connection and solidified community.

Working together in light of what God has to say to and about each of us (Foundation) has made such an incredible difference in how we relate and speak to each other (Filtration). So much so, that other people noticed and expressed how encouraged they are because of the peace between us.

This is an amazing testimony of the mercy and grace of God. Every time I intentionally incorporate the Foundation, Validation, Cooperation, Donation, and Filtration of *Outside Words* I have the opportunity to learn new ways that God's love reaches to us wherever we are.

These are lessons I continue to learn in the other relationship, as well as along the journey of restoration by God's grace.

The relationship mending that is still in progress was benefitted by another person coming along side us to help show the need to make space for more outside words. With this new understanding and an avenue established in the relationship for better communicating, changes have already begun.

For this I express thankfulness to God, to be sure, and to the other person for their sticking it out and owning their part in the situation even as I further own my part. As this process unfolds, I am convinced that he disconnect will resolve as in truth we use our outside words to speak the love of God to one another.

This is a goal for me that I have not yet fully met. Some of my attempts to validate and cooperate with outside words have backfired as my well intended donations have caused this valuable person even more hurt feelings. I have to continually learn from person to person what one considers a blessing and what does not bless them.

Outside Words for Life

Outside Words is not a magic formula for simple and quick fixes for troubled conversations or relationships. I can testify to that all too well. Relationships are hard. What Outside Words can do is provide the platform where change can begin.

In the past I walked, and still on occasion walk away from conversations hurting because of words and attitude expressed either from me or to me. In such instances, there has not been the desired connection and the potential for community has greatly been diminished. This is by no means my desire. You may find yourself experiencing this, too.

In such an event, do not walk, but rather run back to the Foundation of God and seek his immediate Filtration. This retreat does not have to be a big drawn out production. It is a simple internal shift of attitude to one of humbly seeking and calling out to God for help. It can change the tone and direction of the painful conversation even while it is in process.

We can let God's love and wisdom guide us and guard us as we continue to extend God's love to the person or group we are talking to.

Though we may not be extended validation from the other person, we can still leave the conversation validated because of God's love and acceptance for us. This will happen even as he continues to shape us and grow us into his likeness as we continually apply his unconditional love through the practice of outside words with God and with people.

So, these are just a few suggestions of making sure the God Filtration is in place and that it is built on the God Foundation strategy. If it becomes evident that we have stepped away from our Foundation and Filtration strategies, we can return to them every time we notice they are missing.

Looking Ahead

In the final chapter we will discuss an action plan and resources available to get started using outside words in your daily life to simplify conversations, strengthen connections, and solidify community.

May God bless and empower you as you practice clarifying conversation with courageous compassion.

AFTERWORD

MOTIVATION
CURING THE ACHE

Action Plan

So, what do we do now? How do we begin to take action to build the Foundation and Filtration strategies while incorporating Validation, Cooperation, and Donation, the three steps of *Outside Words*?

Hopefully you personalized this book with your own thoughts and feelings along the way as you responded with your whole heart to the material presented. Whether you recorded your interactions in the margins, in the companion Outside Words Journal, or in a simple notebook, take some time to review your notes.

I encourage you to find a friend with whom to learn and practice *Outside Words*. Then branch out by trying this in daily settings such as at the checkout counter at the store, at the automotive repair shop, at work, or around the dinner table at home.

Make notes of the differences you experience and be sure to include where you could use more practice.

Be Careful

One word of caution is that we should not expect people to make room for our outside words. It will probably be helpful to learn some basic phrases to use in conversations where those you validate and cooperate with (by giving space) seem to never run out of ability to fill up the space with themselves, leaving no room for your donation.

Maybe they are operating in a narcissistic manner, or perhaps they are operating out of a deep need in the moment. Either way, it is important to find caring and non-invalidating ways to eventually interrupt the single focus of the discussion and make a way into the conversation.

As we do this in a way that benefits, builds up, and blesses, we will encourage others as we reinforce the validation that opened the conversation.

"Thank you for sharing with me. I appreciate hearing you. Let me take a moment to share some thoughts and feelings I have, too."

"Pardon my interruption. I just want to interject something in response to what you just said."

"Mind if I jump in here for a moment?"

When necessary, it is fairly simple to interject your donation of value into the conversation while still validating the other person. Remember, validation is the one step that continues throughout the entire conversation process.

Cooperation with the other person comes prior to making our own donation. However once the initial donation has been made, the donations from both parties are freely exchanged back and forth.

Often, people are glad to wrap up their thought and make room for yours.

"Oh, sorry to just keep rambling on and on."

It is not unusual to be so full of one emotion or another such as excitement, sadness, or frustration that we just go on and on to the point that we take the conversation hostage. We actually do each other a service when we caringly and respectfully step in and undo the hostage situation so that the conversation has the freedom to flow once again.

Coaching Questions: What About You?

Here is the last opportunity in this book to respond to reflective questions. Do not pass by this opportunity.

How can you begin to incorporate *Outside Words* into your life?

_____

_____

_____

_____

As you practice *Outside Words*, think about your "aha!" moments. What caught your attention? Why ?

_____

_____

_____

_____

Where have you resounded with what you were reading?

_____

_____

_____

_____

Is there any place in your life where my outside words expressed to you in this book resounded within you, giving you outside words for what you have already experienced and already knew was true even though you never put them into words before? If so, write about it?

_____

_____

_____

_____

_____

How has this book validated you?

_____

_____

_____

_____

_____

How has this book cooperated with you?

_____

_____

_____

_____

_____

How has this book donated to you?

_____

_____

_____

_____

_____

How has God used this book to convict you of changes that need to be made in your approach to God and others? Do you need to become a better listener? Is there anything you need to overcome such as timidity, controlling conversations, or inappropriate jest? God is faithful. His conviction is key to drawing us near to him. After you answer these Questions, seek God and allow him to make the needed adjustments in your heart and actions.

_____

_____

_____

_____

_____

Validating You

I pray that this book has validated you as a person of great worth. My goal was to rehearse and reemphasize time and time again the value that you have simply because God decided to make you. God chose to create you in the specific qualities that he did, in the specific time and place for your life. You are a unique and invaluable creation of God.

You can enter into relationship with God no matter what is going on in your life. God has a plan and purpose in your life beyond your struggle, beyond your circumstances, beyond anything you may be going through, or are frustrated with. God has your true identity waiting for you to enter into.

Though this has been written communication, I have kept you in mind and aimed to cooperate with you and give you space throughout the pages of this book to express more of your own outside words to yourself in the extra note pages provided in each chapter.

I have also taken steps to honor you as I use my outside words to donate value to you I have learned and experienced in my life. Even though this is written, I hope that I have considered you and engaged you well.

It was my intention through the Coaching Questions of the "What About You?" sections to engage you with fresh dialogue using your own outside words. Your outside words will begin to be used in new and intentional ways as you agree with points I make or push back in disagreement with them, and even as you dialogue within yourself.

Resources for Outside Words

Practice this process. Team up with someone else and together work on developing and incorporating into your relationship the mindset and skills of *Outside Words*.

One way to reinforce anything you have learned, or to establish any new habit is to teach it to others. Utilize *Outside Words* in your small group gathering at your business, club, church, or school by leading an *Outside Words* Group.

You can simply gather a group of friends to join a book discussion on *Outside Words*. For those wanting to move beyond discussing this process to actually begin practicing it, you can lead a more practical group for *Outside Words*. The options are endless.

You can begin practicing *Outside Words* today in everyday conversations. Practice critiquing each other in your groups. Try using outside words in your texts, when you go to the store, and as you talk to your family and friends.

Most importantly, use *Outside Words* when you pray and talk with God, listening first and foremost.

Further uses for this study would be to engage in *Outside Words* leadership training sessions, conferences, or retreats for your organization or team. Check out our free resources and consider hosting an *Outside Words* event from two to eight hours at your church or business.

Opportunities abound to experience and bless God, be filled with his love, and extend that love to others. When we really find our Foundation in God and receive from him our identity and acceptance, then we can compassionately engage with others whether they accept or reject us. Our security will be from God.

More than this, we can continue to speak truth over others, and bless rather than curse regardless of what comments or attitude they send our way.

This is liberating in two ways. First, we are not defeated by their words or attitudes because our being is secure on the sure Foundation of God. Second, we get to be conduits of God's love and grace as we lovingly speak truth to, but not down to, those with whom we speak.

As you ponder your next steps, I will leave you with this final action step.

Think about any area of your life where you would like to simplify conversation, strengthen connection, and solidify community. Then visit our web page to find out how we can help you begin making the difference you desire.

outsidewordsbook.com

For starters, check out the Outside Words mini course at no cost. This *free* course was designed to get you started on your journey of simplifying conversation, strengthening connection and solidifying community with God and others.

APPENDIX A
OUTSIDE WORDS TO GO

Tweet these quotes from Outside Words. The schedule is provided as a guide. Tweet the quote on the day or during the week listed, or create your own plan.

Example:
"quote of the week goes here" - Debbie Rarick
#OutsideWords #conversation #connection #community #debbierarick #communication #blessdon'tcurse #freedom

January
1 - The human soul aches for genuine conversation that leads to healthy connection and community.
8 - Develop a new way to think
15 - Look into the pain, don't just look past it. Stare it in the face.
22 - Christ is the perfect example of leading by humble submission.
29 - The word of God and its power will be unleashed again and again as we hear and repeat it.

February
5 - Once our words are spoken, we cannot take back their power.

12 - We choose to speak blessings or we choose to speak curses.

19 - Ministry is done for people by people for God's glory.

26 - Elijah the prophet was used to monumental "outside words" from God.

March

4 - Just as God's words shaped creation, our words shape relation.

11 - To understand one another, there needed to be a common system of communication.

18 - Practice "Outside Words" in every conversation, every day, all day long.

25 - I am desperate to improve my ability to hear, understand, process, and respond appropriately when communicating with God.

April

1 - We are not going to understand God or others unless we first invest time and effort to listen.

8 - You cannot change or control another person's thoughts and feelings.

15 - Until we think the thoughts of God, our ways will not be his ways.

22 - God's higher thoughts are expressed in his higher words and evidenced in his higher ways.

29 - Don't just wait on God. Wait with God.

May

6 - Don't become self-sufficient and leave God out of the picture.

13 - The solution for this lingering human longing to reach the heavens could be found, but it would not be based on human effort.

20 - God is calling us to listen to him with the intent to understand him so that we can know him and obey him.

27 - I can validate others by discussing the important things in their lives.

June

3 - We will be filled to the point of overflowing with God's love and acceptance in spite of the struggles on our journey.

10 - I find God more when I am on the beach because I seek God more when I am on the beach.

17 - Begin to think of every group and every single person as the mission field.

24 - I must offer nurture and nourishment for their souls.

31 - Even forgiving in the moment can be quicker than I previously realized.

July

7 - No one processes anything that is denied.

14 - We adorn others with the dignity that God adorns them with.

21 - We cannot truly validate anyone by complimenting what they wear, eat, or drink.

28 - Self must take a step back in order to make room for the other person.

August

4 - God will continue to build my security in him so that I can use my outside words to bless rather than beat down.

11 - We must choose this day and every day who we will serve with our outside words.

18 - Jesus modeled intentional listening to and healthy dependency upon God.

25 - Once a person experiences God wherever they are, they can then grow from there.

September

1 - We will not experience any threat (real or perceived) that is bigger than God's protection.

8 - Consider this, it is more beneficial to spend our time with God prior to when we need what we get from God.

15 - No one can encounter God and remain the same.

22 - Once we hear information from God, we must then seek his instructions.

29 - Authentic personal validation will enable deeper interpersonal connection.

October

6 - I can experience God's peace because one person's misuse of God does not have to rob me of my connection to God.

13 - We can argue with the concept of God, but we must wrestle with the presence of God.

20 - When we are secure in God, we do not need to run down others to try to feel better about ourselves

27 - No matter what, we must keep conversing and connecting.

November

3 - Rightly relating to God enables us to relate in healthy ways to ourselves and to others.

10 - Each time I experience and survive rejection, I further overcome being controlled by the fear of it.

17 - It is not up to other's moods or whims to determine how I relate.

24 - It is painful to back down and give up my right to self-protect.

December

1 - Continue to learn from person to person what is considered a blessing and what does not bless them.

8 - We each have value to add and will do so as we engage and offer of ourselves *to* God *for* others.

15 - Our differences are not to our detriment, but rather to our benefit.

22 - There is no way to donate things of God without first having received God's donation to us.

29 - We must filter our outside words through the filter of Christ.

Sign up at outsidewordsbook.com to get your free print out of *Outside Words* To Go.

Appendix B
Echo the Father

Let my words be few
Let my faith be fueled
Let me seek and hear you, Lord
Let your words be known
Let your will be prayed
On every nation, every shore

And, my heart be broke
By every word you spoke
Other voices fade away
Lord, humbly you start
From your Father's heart
I wait here for you today

Chorus:
Jesus, you hear the Father
Jesus, we long to hear you
Jesus, help us to
Echo you echo the Father

Purify our hearts
So from yours we'll start
To pray with confidence your prayers

OUTSIDE WORDS

Lord, we need your might,
For those you love, we'll fight
To bring your hope to their despair

You are greater still
Confide in us your will
For every circumstance we see
Teach us God, we yearn
Cause our lives to burn
With your passion, Lord, for these

Chorus:
Jesus, you hear the Father
Jesus, we long to hear you
Jesus, help us to
Echo you echo the Father

Bridge:
He hears from God - Authority
We wait for Him - Hear and obey
He transforms us - With purity
We share His words - Come taste and see

Chorus:
Jesus, you hear the Father
Jesus, we long to hear you
Jesus, help us to
Echo you echo the Father

By Debbie Rarick

Sign up at outsidewordsbook.com to request your free chord sheet.

©2016 Debbie Rarick

Appendix C
Risk-lationship©

Life is nowhere else
Life is not by myself
If I don't enter in
Love will not begin
To flow out my heart
But God, I'm afraid to start

Chorus:
What if I fail You
What if I hurt Yours
What if I stumble and fall
Will you still reach me
Please, won't you teach me
How to surrender my all

Relational waters are dangerous
Alive, without assurance
Of desired acceptance, belonging
Still, they are life giving
Relating to You, God, means risking
All that is my being

Chorus
But, what if I fail You
What if I hurt Yours
What if I stumble and fall
Will you still reach me
Please, won't you teach me
How to surrender my all

Bridge:
I want to so badly
To love others righteously
But, I've been so foolish before
I locked up my heart away
Through serving You everyday
But, God, I'm hungry and thirsty for more
So, I'll set free my caged heart
With You I'm beginning to start
Standing in faith full assured
I'll unlock my sheltered soul
And, love others in a way that's whole
'Cause, God Your pure love in me endures

Chorus
But, what if I fail You
What if I hurt Yours
What if I stumble and fall
Will you still reach me
Please, won't you teach me
How to surrender my all

Chorus 2
Lord, I may fail You
Lord, I may hurt Yours
Lord, I may stumble and fall

But, You will still reach me
And, continue to teach me
How to surrender my all

Lord, I surrender my all
Lord, I surrender my all

By Debbie Rarick

Sign up at outsidewordsbook.com to request your free chord sheet.

©2012 Debbie Rarick
All rights reserved.

NOTES

Part 1: The Hurt

Irritation - Talking on Eggshells

1 John 15:13-15
2 Ephesians 1:3-11
3 James 3:1
4 Jantz, Gregory L, PhD, Hope, Help & Healing for Eating Disorders; WaterBrook Press, Colorado Springs, 2010, 69.
5 Galatians 5:22-23

Formation - Speaking With Power

6 Genesis 1
7 Herzog, David, Courts of Heaven,
8 Ephesians 5:21
9 Philippians 2:5-8
10 Covey, Steven R., The 7 Habits of Highly Effective People: Powerful Lessons in Personal Change; Simon & Schuster, New York, 1989, 237.
11 Venter, Yan G., Dr., *The Broken Branch: an orphan epidemic; 52.*
12 Prince, Derek, *War in Heaven: Taking Your Place in the Epic Battle with Evil; Chosen Books, Bloomington, Minnesota, 2016, 147.*
13 Romans 12:1-2
14 Numbers 13-14
15 Numbers 14:1
16 Genesis 25:29-34
17 Genesis 25:32
18 Genesis 25:27

19   Genesis 1:27-28
20   2 Corinthians 5
21   John 12:49, John 14:10
22   Echo the Father, see Appendix B
23   Romans 10:13
24   Romans 10:9
25   Ephesians 4:29
26   John 17
27   Ephesians 3-5

Part 2: The Hope

Communication - Hearing and Being Heard
28   Covey, Stephen R., The 7 Habits of Highly Effective People: Powerful Lessons in Personal Change; Simon & Schuster, New York, 1989, 235-260.
29   Ibid., 238
30   Merriam-Webster

Implementation - Thinking and Feeling
31   Goleman, Daniel, Emotinal Intelligence: Why it Can Matter More than IQ; Bantam Books, New York, 1995.
32   Deuteronomy 6:5
33   Matthew 22:37; Mark 12:30; Luke 10:27
34   Blue Letter Bible Lexicon, blueletterbible.com
35   Ibid.
36   Zacharias, Ravi, Does God Favor a Gender?: Ravai Zacharias at the University of Kentucky, https://www.youtube.com/watch?v=MD3CsFfLxlo
37   Ibid.
38   Celebrate Recovery; See: celebraterecovery.com
39   Celebrate Recovery Participant Guide 1
40   See: Isaiah 55:9
41   Genesis 1:3
42   John 19:30
43   Ephesians 4:8
44   James 5:17
45   James 5:18

46 Philippians 2:5-8
47 James 4:10
48 James 4:6; 1 Peter 5:5

Part 3: The Help

Foundation - The Beginning With God Strategy
49 John 10:10
50 Ibid.
51 John 17
52 John 17:1
53 John 17:15
54 John 17:17
55 John 17:21
56 See Appendix a for Echo the Father, the song
57 Ecclesiastes 3:11
58 Romans 10:9
59 Deuteronomy 6:4
60 Romans 10:13
61 Romans 10:9-10
62 Matthew 7:7
63 Ephesians 4 -5
64 Jeremiah 29:12-13
65 John 3:16
66 John 10:3, 14
67 James 1:17
68 Romans 5:1-5
69 John 17:20-23
70 Matthew 5:14
71 vocabulary.com/dictionary/assimilation
72 Warren, Rick, The Purpose Driven Life.
73 James 4:8
74 Psalm 91:1 King James Version
75 Sorge, Bob, Secrets of the Secret Place: Keys to Igniting Your Personal Time with God; Oasis House, Grandview.

Validation - Simplify Conversation, Step One
76 Ephesians 5:29

77 Ephesians 1:1-11

78 Jeremiah 6:14, The Living Bible

79 Jeremiah 6:14

80 Luke 18:1-8

81 Covey, Stephen R., The 7 Habits of Highly Effective People: Powerful Lessons in Personal Change; Simon & Schuster, New York, 1989, 185-203.

82 Matthew 6:25-34

83 Ephesians 1:17

84 Ephesians 1:18-19

85 Ephesians 1:21

86 Ephesians 1:22-23

87 Ephesians 2:1-3

88 Ephesians 2:4-5

89 Ephesians 2:6-7

90 Ephesians 3:17

91 Matthew 6:33

Cooperation - Strengthen Connection, Step Two

92 Ephesians 3:16

93 Ephesians 3:17

94 Covey, Steven R., The 7 Habits of Highly Effective People: Powerful Lessons in Personal Change; Simon & Schuster, New York, 1989, 235 - 260.

95 Philippians 4:7

96 Psalm 91:1, King James Version

97 John 7:38

98 Proverbs 3:5

99 John 3:16-18

100 John 3:18

Donation - Solidify Community, Step Three

101 Covey, Steven R., The 7 Habits of Highly Effective People: Powerful Lessons in Personal Change; Simon & Schuster, New York, 1989, 235 - 260.

102 Kiyosaki, Robert, T.; with Sharon L Lechter, C.P.A., Rich Dad: The Business School for People Who Like Helping People; Momentum Media, Lake Dallas, Texas, 68.

103 Ibid., 69.
104 Luke 19:11-26
105 See Appendix B for Risk-lationship, the song
106 Romans 12:1-2
107 Kiyosaki, 71.
108 Seamands, David A., Healing for Damaged Emotions; Cook Communications, Colorado Springs, Colorado, 9-10.
109 Ephesians 5:1

Filtration - The Ending With God Strategy
110 Proverbs 17:22
111 Ephesians 4:29
112 Psalm 39:1
113 Ephesians 5:1-4
114 Matthew 25:40,45
115 Vallotton, Kris, and Johnson, Bill, The Supernatural Ways of Royalty; Destiny Image Publishers, Shippensburg, PA, 21.
116 Psalm 34:8

Acknowledgements

With deepest appreciation I lift gratitude to God for the individuals and business owners who supported this project faithfully for years as it developed. *Outside Words* was made possible through this generosity. My heart warms with awe and wonder. May God bless you a thousand times over.

Appreciation must be expressed to the past and present Board members, supporters, and volunteers of You See Me Free Ministries. I am grateful to be part of this amazing team of men and women willing to serve for others. The work you do matters greatly and impacts lives and eternities of individuals and families more than you may realize.

This effort was greatly enhanced by my family members and friends who served as encouragers, prayers, and proofreaders. You provided encouragement, hope, and invaluable feedback in the form of compliments and critique. You shed light and gave much needed guidance along the way. You have enhanced this book.

Media services and products in the making of Outside Words were provided by Enzo Scorziello of FireCloud Studio, and Corey Engel of Esotechnics. Thank you each for pouring into me and this book.

Stephanie Butts, Wendy Davis, and Darlene Vise, your skills and diverse editing styles contributed valuable suggestions and solutions. Your friendships and sacrifices for this book are recognized and relished.

Expertise offered by Kary Oberbrunner and his team at Author Academy Elite equipped this book publishing journey non-stop. Their instruction and assistance, along with the fellowship of the Igniting Souls Tribe together provided the desired coaching and community on this journey. May you never burn out.

Ultimately, I acknowledge and praise God in gratitude for his choice to pursue conversation, connection, and community with me. May this book glorify God, and lead many to deeper relationship and more outside words with Jesus, or to begin such relationship and conversation with him. Thank you, God, for your consideration of and continued transformation of my life through the Holy Spirit.

—Debbie Rarick

Your Next Steps

Visit outsidewordsbook.com to request your free resources.

Free *Outside Words* Resources

- *Outside Words* Journal
- *Outside Words* Mini Course
- *Outside Words* To Go - Tweet Schedule

Continue the Conversation

Bring alive your business or organization with the tried and proven strategies and steps of *Outside Words*.

Bring Dr. Debbie Rarick to present at your next event.

Other *Outside Words* Services

- **Personal or Group Coaching**
- **Certification for *Outside Words* Team**
- **Leadership Training**
- **Retreats**
- **Workshops**
- **Conferences**
- **Speaking**

ABOUT THE AUTHOR

D r. Debbie Rarick is an author, communicator, and coach who has used her outside words to teach, preach, and lead group ministry and worship for more than two decades. During her studies at George W. Truett Theological Seminary, she founded You See Me Free Ministries in 2005, through which she helps individuals organizations find reconciliation, rest and recovery so they can be free to excel in their purpose and potential.

Debbie is a Certified Christian Life Coach, and a Trainer and Coach for both the Your Secret Name and The Deeper Path Coaching Programs. She is based in Waco, Texas where she has served in several churches in various administrative and ministry positions. She enjoys resting, laughing, learning music, traveling, yard work, and community.

Connect with Debbie at outsidewords@debbierarick.com

Invite Dr. Rarick to coach your leadership, ministry, or volunteer team.